The London That
Never Happened

The image on the cover was perhaps the most dramatic of various designs for a brand new Camden Town station around the year 2000, featuring an over-site development that resembled an alien spaceship having landed. It was dramatic, but would have faced opposition from residents.

This book includes some images from the wonderful Creative Commons resource and the author's own collection.

The following pages use images from the Capital History library: 14/15, 17, 18, 25, 31, 32, 33, 43.

For other illustrations we are grateful to:
Alamy 11
Tim Demuth 13
Peter Figg 34/35, 70 top, 75, 82
Foster+Partners 78, 79
Getty Images 45
The Guardian 60, 61
London Underground Ltd cover, 84, 85
Chris Marshall, www. roads.org.uk 71, 72/73.
RIBA 54 bottom, 74
Richard Rogers 80, 81
TfL 92, 93, 95

First Published 2022

Published by Capital History
www.capitalhistory.co.uk

Printed by Parksons Graphics

© Capital History and Antony Badsey-Ellis 2022

Contents

National Monument to Isaac Newton	5
The Trafalgar Square pyramid	6
The Crystal Palace Tower	8
The Wembley Park Tower	10
The Morgan Tubes	12
St Paul's Bridge	14
Aldwych to South Bank Bridge	18
The London Goods Clearing House	19
The Kearney Tubes	22
New roads for London: the early 1900s	24
The Underground Goods Railway	26
King's Cross airport	30
The Charing Cross Bridge	32
Peckham Thames	34
The "Tideless Thames" barrage	36
Revitalizing the South Bank	38
The Charing Cross heliport	42
High Paddington	44
The Post-WWII road schemes	46
Monorails to Heathrow	50
The Monster of Piccadilly Circus	52
Roads below	56
The City of London Pedways	60
Plans for Westminster	62
Redevelopment of Soho	66
Covent Garden rebuilding	67
The Marylebone Busway	68
The Ringways	70
London monorails	76
Hammersmith Broadway redevelopment	78
The National Gallery Extension	80
The Thames Gateway Bridge	82
Camden Town station	84
The Financial District	86
Battersea Power Station	90
The Garden Bridge	92
The Cross-River Tram	94

Introduction

In a city the size of London, the only constant is change – new buildings and new infrastructure to support the changing population and its needs. Not every plan comes to fruition though. The planning process influences this, by providing the opportunity for people to register their views on new developments, and to consider developments in a wider context. Sometimes new buildings are approved, but the money to build them isn't forthcoming, or the economic situation changes.

Some of the earliest schemes for unbuilt London date back to the aftermath of the Great Fire of 1666. Architects including Sir Christopher Wren proposed using the wholesale demolition of much of the City of London as an opportunity to build wide, straight roads with large squares and piazzas where they met. Unfortunately the complexities of land ownership and the urgent need to rebuild meant that the layout of the City remained much the same after the new buildings were constructed.

There can be many reasons why new structures aren't built, but the fact that this happens means that there is a rich pool of ideas to be explored. This book brings together a selection of them, from the mid-Victorian era through to the twenty-first century. The vast number of proposed schemes means that it can only feature a small proportion, and the selection here is an eclectic mix. They date from around the start of the Victorian period; the Trafalgar Square pyramid, although proposed in 1815, could not have been built until the site of the square was cleared in the 1830s. I haven't included the 1840 Metropolitan Improvement plan, the many proposals contained within the eight volumes of the Royal Commission on London Traffic reports, dating from 1905, nor the London Plans of 1943 and 1944. Much of these schemes focused on new roads, and I have tried to find a balance of schemes.

Large-scale schemes that were obviously impossible have not been included. The MARS Plan, developed in the 1930s and first published in 1942, proposed nothing short of the complete replacement of greater London. In its place would have been 14 residential strips, perpendicular to the Thames, with seven on each side. This was obviously completely unfeasible, even without the dire financial straits that the UK was in after the Second World War.

The genesis of this book was a talk that I was invited to give at the London Transport Museum in late 2019, as part of the launch of their superb *Hidden London* exhibition. I have added many more schemes to those that I described that evening in order to write this book. I am very grateful to Miranda Schiller at the LT Museum for that invite, as it has led to fascinating research into some of London's forgotten stories. Thanks also go to the historian and presenter Tim Dunn for a couple of suggestions that I hadn't previously seen, and to Chris Marshall for the use of his Ringway maps (www.roads.org.uk). The staff of the National Archives and the London Metropolitan Archives have also helped, during the difficult period of the Covid pandemic, in finding the original records that I have used in the research. Jim Whiting from Capital Transport has located many of the illustrations and maps, as well as suggesting some of the subjects.

My final thanks go, as ever, to my wife Wendy and my sons for putting up with my disappearances to carry out the research and writing necessary to compile a book such as this.

I hope that you enjoy your exploration of the London that Never Happened as much as I did!

Antony Badsey-Ellis, Amersham, March 2022

National Monument to Isaac Newton

Possibly one of the most unusual structures proposed for London was a monument to Sir Isaac Newton. The idea, made in 1834, was to construct a large flat-topped pyramid around Newton's house, which still stood in St Martin's Street, between Leicester and Trafalgar Squares. The house would be contained in a domed chamber inside the pyramid, and the whole structure would be topped by a large globe. The globe was to be about as tall as the house, and the pyramid would take up a similar area to St Paul's Cathedral.

The monument was suggested nine years earlier by Thomas Steele, of Magdalene College in Cambridge, who described his idea in an anonymous letter to *The Times*.[1] He was inspired by the Franciscan chapel housed within the Papal Basilica of Saint Mary of the Angels in Assisi, and suggested that the house be fitted up to contain a council chamber and library for the Royal Society. His letter concluded that the structure would protect the house so that it "might stand fast for ages, a British monument more sublime than the Pyramids". This letter described the house being enclosed in a circular tower with the globe on top.

He continued to refine his idea, because in 1834 he commissioned an artist to create the picture and cross-section shown here. By this time, the circular tower had been replaced by a stepped pyramid.

The monument was never built, and Newton's house was demolished in 1913.

A cross-section of the proposed monument, showing Newton's house within the domed chamber.

The Trafalgar Square pyramid

The year is 1815, and England has come out as the victor in the Napoleonic Wars. Something needs to be built to mark this auspicious event, and for Colonel Frederick Trench, MP, what could be better than a pyramid? The campaign from 1798-1801 had left its mark on English society, raising the profile and popularity of all things Egyptian. Trench proposed the construction of a stepped pyramid the same height as St Paul's Cathedral (364 ft) to celebrate the Battle of the Nile, which would have filled the central part of what became Trafalgar Square. The pyramid would have one step for each year of the wars (22 in total), with each tier being decorated with a carved stone frieze.

The square that is now dominated by Nelson's Column did not exist in 1815; it was the site of the King's Mews. It was not until 1826 that the site began to be cleared to form the square, and by this time Trench's idea had faded away.

At the time that Trench suggested his pyramid, Admiral Nelson had yet to attain the popularity that later led to the column being raised, and the Battle of the Nile was seen as more significant than that of Trafalgar. The cost was estimated at £1 million: perhaps not much today, but at the time this was 1% of Government spending. Trench thought that the large number of men being discharged from the military (due to the end of the wars) would be able to help with the construction, which might take around five years.

Trench was assisted in his design by the architects Philip and Matthew Cotes Wyatt, with the designs being exhibited at the home of the Duke of York in Pall Mall. Despite the publicity, his idea went nowhere. The site was cleared and named Trafalgar Square in around 1835, and Nelson's Column was completed in 1843.

How the pyramid might have appeared today, occupying Trafalgar Square in place of Nelson's Column.

How the view from Whitehall would have been like had the pyramid been built.

The Crystal Palace Tower

The wonder of 1851 was the Great Exhibition, created under the patronage of Prince Albert, and located in Hyde Park in a revolutionary glass building. Designed by Joseph Paxton, who was subsequently knighted for his part in the Exhibition, it was constructed from a standardized set of cast iron sections with panes of glass fitted to ensure the maximum amount of light. It was constructed faster, and more cheaply, than was expected when the Exhibition was proposed, and the modular design allowed a single workman to install over 100 panes of glass per day. In total, over 290,000 panes were used, with around 4,000 tonnes of iron.

The building, and the Exhibition, were a great success, but were intended to be temporary. Six months had been allowed for the Exhibition to run, and after it closed the debate began on what to do with the building.

An architect called Charles Burton proposed dismantling it and reconfiguring the components to create a tower. No specific site was identified in the original description, published in *The Builder*, other than stating that it would be nearby. This would have addressed concerns about the amount of Hyde Park covered by the Crystal Palace (almost 72,000 m^2).

The tower would have been enormously high: at 1,000 feet it would have been almost as tall as today's Shard, at London Bridge. The design consisted of a series of concentric towers, with the inner towers given support from the outer towers. The tallest tower would have been octagonal in plan, rising the full height of 1,000 feet. Around this would have been a decagonal (10-sided) tower, to 840 feet, with this surrounded by a 12-sided tower up to 660ft. These would be contained within a square tower with sides 120 ft long up to a height of 440 feet, with turrets at each corner and a large clock at the top of each side. A larger square tower to 198 feet would come next, with covered galleries running along each side at the top.

Within the tower, visitors would be able to ascend using what were termed 'ascending rooms' mounted on 'vertical railways': what we would call a lift. Just four were felt to be sufficient, and they would allow the public to see the views from the different levels, as well as examine the contents of the fifty floors. The tower was intended to follow on from the Great Exhibition by forming a "depository of every branch of art and manufacture our own kingdom produces", together with a selection of exhibits from around the world.

Whilst this would have been an amazing site, despite the approval of the original engineers of the Crystal Palace, it would not have been practical. The materials required to build a tower of this size did not exist in the 1850s, and the tower would never have been completed. The cast iron would just have been too brittle to cope with the stresses of a skyscraper, and it would have collapsed under its own weight.

A contemporary illustration of the Crystal Palace Tower, showing how it would have dominated the view from miles around. It isn't clear where this is meant to be; although the report suggested that it would be in Hyde Park, this would appear to be somewhere more suburban.

The Wembley Park Tower

In 1889, a large metal tower opened in Paris as part of the Great Exhibition held there. Designed by Gustave Eiffel, it was a great success, and nearly recouped its costs from ticket sales during the exhibition. This sparked an idea across the Channel in the mind of Sir Edward Watkin, the Chairman of the Metropolitan Railway, who thought that London also needed a tower.

He first asked Eiffel if he would be interested, but was gently turned down, Eiffel stating "If I, after erecting my Tower on French soil, were to erect one in England, they would not think me so good a Frenchman as I hope I am". Watkin instead held a competition, inviting designs for a tower with a prize of 500 guineas for the winning entry. The successful design would be erected on the high ground at Wembley, on an estate purchased by the Metropolitan Railway. Watkin could see the sale of railway tickets as well as tickets up the tower.

Sixty-eight designs were received, several from overseas, and the winning design was submitted by the London architects A.D. Stewart, J.M. McLaren, and W. Dunn. It bore a reasonably close resemblance to the Eiffel Tower, but it was taller – an important piece of one-upmanship over the French. At 366 m tall it would not only have been higher than the Paris structure (324 m), but over 10% taller than The Shard, at London Bridge. Of all the designs though, it was one of the shortest: the tallest, submitted by a French architect, was to rise to a height of 700 m.

It was also one of the saner designs. There was a tower topped by an enormous wrought-iron globe; a tower intended to form an "aerial colony"; one with four "captive parachutes" on which daring visitors could descend; towers with spiral railways and tramways to ascend and descend; and, possibly the most alarming of all, one in which the lifts would be blown to the top of the tower using compressed air.

Work started in 1891 with the construction of foundations, but already there were clouds on the horizon. The Tower Company, Limited had been formed to run the competition, raise the money, and build the tower, and it was the second of these that was the problem. Work started before all of the money had been found, and economies crept in from the start. The six legs on which the winning design was placed were reduced to four even before the foundations were started, and *The Times* noted that the tower "will not be constructed in strict accordance with any of the designs, all being … of a more expensive character than the circumstances warrant".[2]

The metal sections for the tower were brought from the ironworks in Manchester via temporary sidings laid from the nearby Metropolitan Railway to the construction site, and slowly the first stage of the tower began to be assembled. This was completed and opened to the public in May 1894, but did not attract the visitor numbers that had been hoped for. The Tower Company seemed surprised that people were not particularly enthusiastic to view Wembley from a height of 155 ft. Ticket sales brought in a little money, but it was estimated that the company had only £15,000 remaining, and yet to complete the tower some £200,000 would be required.

The tower remained a rusting hulk on the Wembley skyline for just twelve years. In 1906 workmen moved in to demolish it. They started by using sledgehammers to remove the bolts and rivets, which allowed some of the metal girders to be taken down. The following year, with just the legs remaining, a mining explosive called roburite was placed around them and the last vestiges of the tower removed.

The site of the tower is very easy to spot, even today: it was located on the spot now occupied by Wembley Stadium.

The Wembley Park Tower never went above the first level, but this attractive image of the pleasure grounds, published by the Metropolitan Railway, shows how it would have appeared when completed.

The Morgan Tubes

London in the early 1900s was the scene of a fierce rivalry between two American financiers. One was Charles Tyson Yerkes, who had made (and then lost) a fortune in Philadelphia, and then made a new fortune from running public transportation in Chicago. The other was John Pierpont Morgan, the New York banker and financier who made his fortune on Wall Street.

In 1901, Morgan began his interest in London tube railways, providing backing to two railways called the Piccadilly & City (P&CR), and the North East London Railway (NELR). The P&CR was intended to form an eastward extension of the Brompton & Piccadilly Circus Railway (B&PCR) from Piccadilly Circus to Cannon Street, and the NELR was then to continue the line to Tottenham and Walthamstow. The B&PCR objected to the P&CR plans, as they had their own eastward extension (to Angel, Islington) planned.

The problem of the connection was solved the following year, when Morgan agreed to purchase a half-share in the new London United Electric Railway (LUER) – yet another planned tube railway, this time linking Hammersmith and Charing Cross. The LUER included a separate line from Marble Arch to Clapham Junction, with passenger interchange between the two at Knightsbridge. The promoters of the LUER were the London United Tramways company, which had an extensive network of tram routes in west London, converging on Hammersmith and Shepherd's Bush. The London County Council forbade any further extension of the trams towards London, and so the LUER scheme was born.

By combining the LUER with his other two railways, Morgan envisaged single railway stretching from Hammersmith to Palmers Green. The LUER agreed to drop the section of their line east of Hyde Park Corner, and the P&CR (which had put forward a plan to build its own route to Hammersmith in 1902) was amended to join the LUER at the same point. The promotors explained to the Parliamentary Committee that was considering the tube railway bills in 1902 that they considered their railways to be one complete scheme. This would involve the operation of trains along the full length of the route without the need to change, or hold separate tickets for different sections. With the LUER as part of this arrangement, through ticketing with the LUT was also planned. The Managing Director of the LUT claimed that this scheme offered "the only true solution of the burning question of the hour – the relief of overcrowded London".

The Committee made some minor changes to the plans. A large loop at the west end, serving both Shepherd's Bush and Hammersmith, was removed after concerns over the underground junction that would be required. At the other end of the line, the section from Southgate to Palmers Green was deleted as it would have interfered with a cricket pitch – definitely not acceptable in England!

It was clear to the Parliamentary Committee that approving both the Yerkes and Morgan proposals would result in needless duplication of routes. There were already many examples of this on the main-line railways, due in part to the laissez-faire approach taken by the Government through the lack of any centralized planning of routes. Counsel for Yerkes noted that the B&PCR was already approved; his counterpart for Morgan argued that no work had been done, and so the line was clearly intended to thwart other railways in Parliament. As if to disprove this, the Board of the B&PCR immediately ordered construction to start. The company and its supporters continued to argue that authorizing another railway to run under the same streets for almost two miles (Sloane Street to Piccadilly Circus) was fundamentally wrong.

Morgan's tube railway scheme was approved by the Committee in July 1902, so long as it was constructed in its entirety. This did not seem to be a problem, but it was the detail that led to the unravelling of the scheme. The problem arose when the LUT pushed for equal control of the railways (they had originally been allocated three-eighths).

Morgan refused to budge, and his inclusion of a fourth railway in the group without asking the LUT had caused further unhappiness. Although the length of route contributed by the LUER was less than half, the LUT argued that their trams would bring a large number of passengers onto the line, and that they also had considerable engineering and transport operating experience.

After their request for an equal stake was rejected a second time, in August, the LUT Chairman was furious, and (perhaps in a fit of pique) decided to sell all of his shares in the company. This might not have been a problem, except that they were sold to the bankers who were financing the Yerkes tubes. When the bill for the Morgan tubes came back before Parliament in October, the LUT withdrew the section of line between Sloane Street and Hyde Park Corner, on the grounds that it would duplicate the B&PCR (which was now part of the same company), and would be an expensive section. Eight days later, the entire LUER Bill was withdrawn.

Parliament was not happy. The House of Lords described the actions of the LUT as a breach of faith with the Morgan group, and more seriously, with Parliament itself. Despite a series of attempts to patch the scheme up so that it would meet the requirement for the line to be built in its entirety, it was decided that this would be without precedent in Parliament. Morgan's plans to control a good chunk of London's tube railways were in ruins. Morgan commented that the actions of his rivals were the "greatest rascality and conspiracy I ever heard of", which Yerkes might well have taken as a compliment!

This is how the Underground map may have looked in 1910 if Morgan had won the battle to build new London tubes at the start of the 20th Century. It shows the 'Piccadilly, City & North East Railway' (Hammersmith to Southgate), the 'London United Electric Railway' (Marble Arch to Clapham Junction), and the 'City & North East Suburban Electric Railway' (Monument to Waltham Abbey). Together they were promoted as the London Suburban Railway.

St Paul's Bridge

The increase in vehicular traffic in the early years of the twentieth century led to a number of suggestions for improvements to existing roads, and the construction of completely new roads. A combination of both was the plan for St Paul's Bridge and its connecting roads. This was to be a new 80-ft-wide bridge over the Thames between the existing Blackfriars and Southwark Bridges, with three arches across the river. It was proposed by the Bridge House Estates, the body that maintained many of London's bridges, and in 1909 was estimated to cost just over £1.5 million.[3] One of the attractions of the new bridge was that it would be able to accommodate a tram route from south London up to Cannon Street.

Its southern approach would lead into the Old Kent Road, heading south-eastwards to Dover. On the north bank it would cross Upper Thames Street and Queen Victoria Street on a viaduct, to end at Cannon Street. Basil Mott was the engineer who planned the work, and he also suggested that it would be useful to continue the road north past St Paul's Cathedral to Aldersgate Street. A tramway subway would be included, allowing double-deck trams to run underground from Cannon Street to the tramways further north, on Goswell Road, without running into (or causing) congestion at Cheapside.

The plan was tied up with other plans to rebuild Southwark Bridge, which was felt to be too narrow and was approached on steep gradients. It therefore needed reconstruction, regardless of whether a new bridge was built, and money was set aside for this work as well.

In 1910 a dispute arose with the Royal Institute of British Architects, who asked if the bridge could be aligned with the dome of St Paul's Cathedral, which would open up a vista from the south bank. The Corporation of the City of London, which oversaw the Bridge House Estates, estimated that this change would add £1 million to the cost, and so refused. The general feeling seemed to be that the bridge had been designed by engineers without

A contemporary drawing of how the St Paul's Bridge might have appea[red]

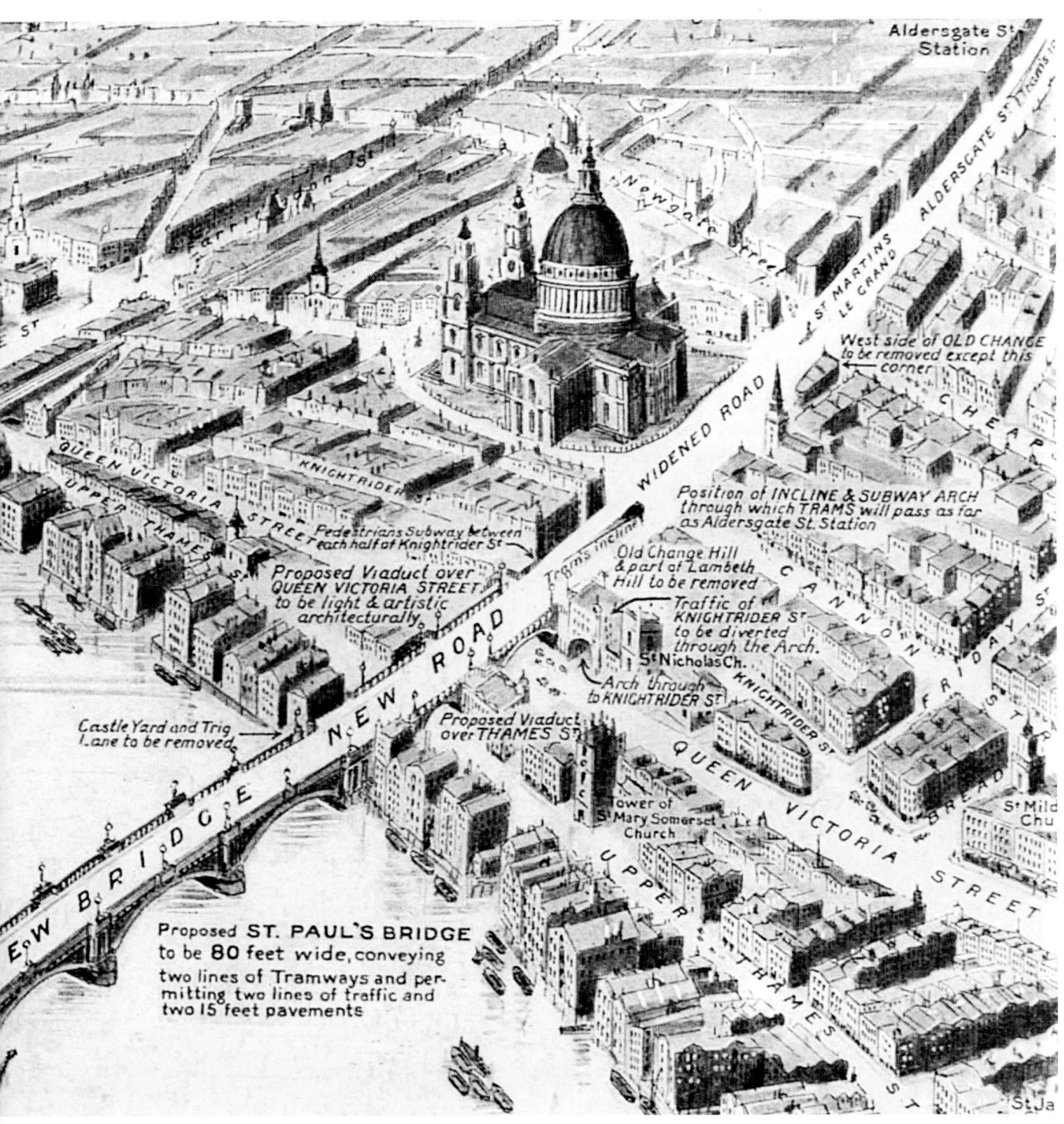

the 1909 scheme come to pass.

any input from architects, and given the prestigious location it was essential to have an architect involved. This led to some interesting debate about whether the south face of the cathedral was designed by Wren to be seen from a distance, or if it was too plain.

Meetings and occasional letters in the press rumbled on throughout the year, with the RIBA feeling that a one-off opportunity was being missed, and threatening to lodge objections to the Bill for the work when it came before Parliament the following year.[4] One unusual feature of the RIBA proposal was that their bridge would be a skew bridge, crossing the river on a diagonal path, but with the two river piers parallel to the flow of the water.

Through 1911 the Bill was considered by Parliament and its committees, with evidence being heard for and against the scheme. The promoters agreed to engage architects to work on the design, leaving the argument about the alignment to continue. Concerns were voiced about the stability of the southern side of the Cathedral, were the new street to finish there, and those in favour of the original proposal noted that a skew bridge would be very complex to build in stone, and so steel or concrete would have to be used, to the detriment of the bridge's appearance. After due process, the Corporation of London (Bridges) Act was passed in 1911, giving authority for the bridge to be built.[5] The Ministry of Transport agreed to provide some funding towards the road improvements either side of the river, and the London Country Council voted to allocate up to £350,000 because of the tramway.

In late 1913 a competition was announced for the design of the bridge. The following June, Mr G Washington Browne, and Edinburgh architect, won the £300 first prize for his five-arched stone bridge. Pylons and obelisks were placed at each end of the bridge, described in *The Times* as "mere excrescences made up of architectural features and utterly incongruous with the structure of the bridge". In their review of the competition, they felt that many of the entrants had focused on architectural flourishes at the expense of the engineering – rather ironic given the concerns expressed in 1909 about the original scheme. Washington Browne's design was not adopted as submitted, but instead was modified with elements from the second-placed design, most notably the covered walkways for pedestrians along both sides of the bridge.

The First World War intervened before any work could start, and for the duration of the conflict the only activity was the extension of the time limit for building the bridge. Once the war was over, it was 1920 before consideration was given to the scheme, in part as a potential project to help relieve unemployment.[6] However, the City Corporation was beginning to have its doubts. Although it had purchased almost 100 properties needed, some of the Bridge House Estates Committee were not convinced that it was still the right plan for London. Nonetheless, they succeeded in getting a new Act of Parliament in 1921 allowing further time to complete the bridge.

A related matter arose in 1924: Waterloo Bridge, which had been receiving repairs for some years, was found to have serious subsidence on three adjacent piers, and was closed on 11 May for fears that the condition could rapidly get worse if traffic continued over it.[7] The bridge, designed by the architect John Rennie, was viewed by many as a masterpiece, and a decade of dithering occurred whilst the authorities tried to decide what to do. In the meantime, Waterloo was a busy bridge, already too narrow for the traffic that was now being displaced, whereas the scheme for St Paul's Bridge was not in a congested part of London but would consume funds that could be used to relieve congestion elsewhere.

The creation by the Government of an Advisory Board on London Traffic gave the Corporation of London the opportunity to pass the problem on to another body. In May 1924, the London County Council announced an inquiry into road traffic across the Thames, and this too gave an opportunity to defer the decision. The resultant Royal Commission into Cross-River Traffic in London was not in favour of the St Paul's Bridge scheme. Attempts were made to keep the plan alive, most notably by a 1928 proposal to route

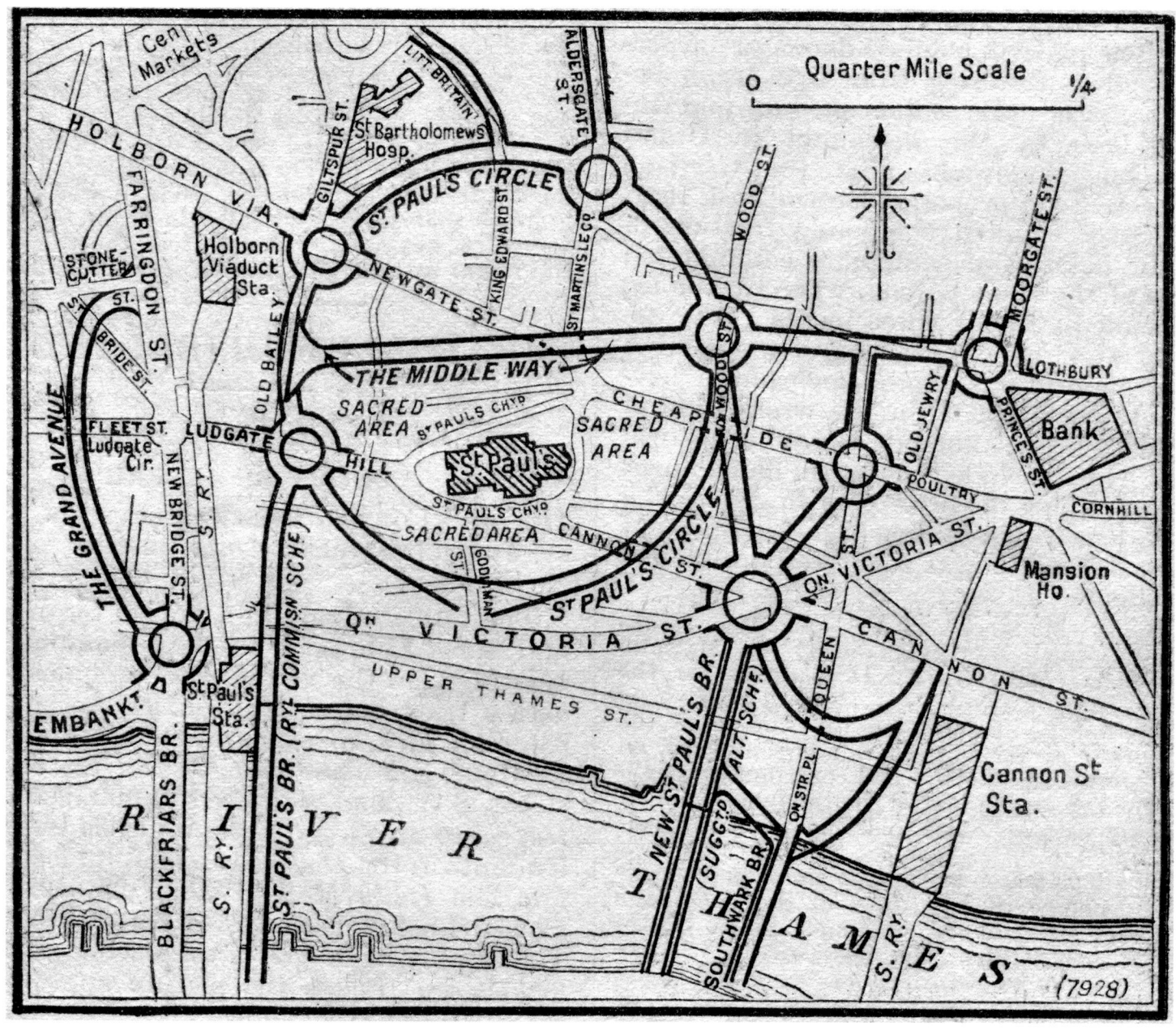

A plan published in 1928 showing the two possible locations for the St Paul's Bridge, together with proposals for significant changes to the roads around the Cathedral to improve traffic flow in the City.

the northern approach further to the east, away from the Cathedral, so as to remove the objections from the cathedral surveyor who was extremely worried about the effect of traffic vibration on the building. This did not satisfy the cathedral authorities, and on 12 October the Common Council of the City Corporation rejected the plans for the bridge. However, this did not prevent a request to Parliament to provide another extension of time.

In February 1929, the third bill to extend the life of the scheme was rejected by Parliament, bringing to an end the long-running saga of St Paul's Bridge.

Aldwych to South Bank Bridge

A new bridge was suggested in 1910 to improve communications across the Thames. Like Waterloo Bridge a little to the west, it would connect the Strand on the north bank with Waterloo on the south. A pair of pedestrian lifts would be provided at each end, descending to embankment level. The roadway would include tracks for trams to use, which would descend into tunnel on the approach to the Strand and curve under the Aldwych to link in with the recently completed Kingsway tram subway.

Somerset House and King's College would have formed an island bounded by the Strand, the Thames, and the norther approaches to the two bridges, and the entrance to Temple Underground station would have been beneath the new bridge.

Drawings such as this were staple fare for newspapers, journals, and books of the time. Minutely detailed, they showed readers how new structures might appear. The lift towers can be seen at each end of the bridge, and the tram subway entrance is in the upper right corner.

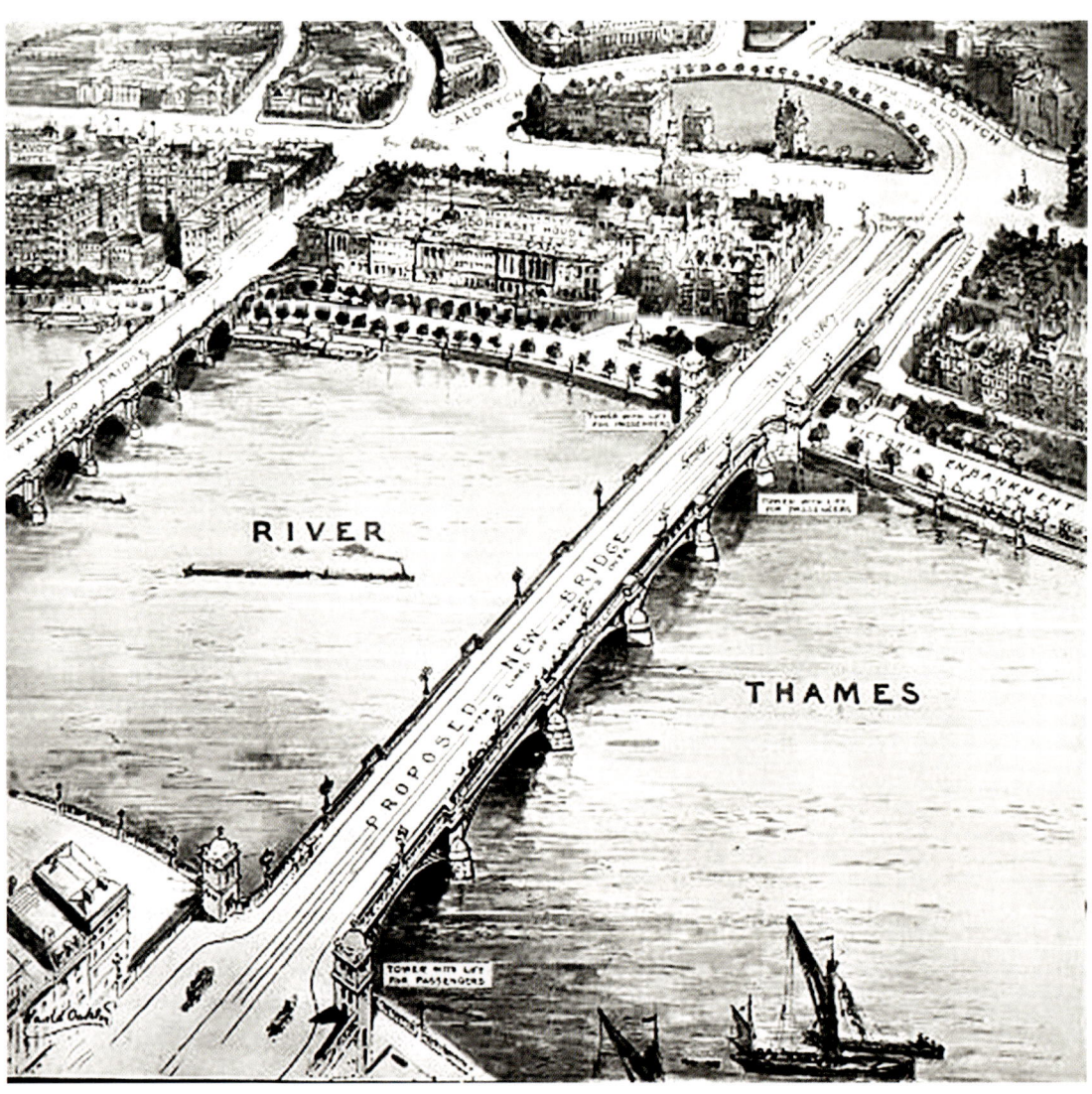

The London Goods Clearing House

Alfred Gattie was an engineer who was ahead of his time. Noting how much time was wasted by goods being transported between places (and often sitting idle in vehicles), in 1910 he proposed a central clearing house for goods in London.[8] This would be, in essence, a warehouse. It would, however, be big – the largest building in the world, in fact. Taking up the block of land between the Farringdon Road and St John Street, and with the Clerkenwell Road running through the middle on an east/west axis, it was designed to have the widest possible access from main roads. Importantly, it would be served at basement level by rail as the Metropolitan Railway, together with its City Widened lines used by several main-line companies, already cut across the proposed site.

As well as road and rail, water transport was also proposed. Gattie wanted to reopen Bridge Wharf, at Blackfriars at the mouth of the covered Fleet River. A jetty built at the widened mouth of the Fleet would allow goods to be transferred to and from boats here. Between the wharf and the warehouse, the existing railway line would be used.

The warehouse itself would have been immense. Some 1,300 feet long, and 440 ft wide, it would occupy an area similar to Lord's cricket ground (or seven times the area of St Paul's Cathedral). From sub-basement to roof its height was to 180 ft, but its water towers would reach to a height of 200 ft above street level. These were to hold 1½ million gallons of water feeding a sprinkler system, enabling the warehouse to deal with fires. Some 3 million square feet of floor area would be spread over six floors in the building, which was designed by the architect R. Stephen Ayling. It would have a steel frame and be built of reinforced concrete to help make it fire-proof.

Below street level, 28 railway sidings would have space for 1,000 trucks and wagons. Below, in the sub-basement, would be storage for goods containers. This was another new concept, and about 50 years ahead of its time. Gattie foresaw the need for a standard size of container that could

A view of the freight warehouse, with a cutaway to show the railway sidings beneath and a plane coming in to land on the roof.

easily be handled by standardized equipment.

So why the need for such an enormous warehouse? Gattie noted the success of the Bankers' Clearing House in saving effort transferring funds between banks. Instead of each bank having to physically transfer money to each other bank with whom they had done business, each just made one transaction with the Clearing House, which reconciled all of the transactions and ensured that everyone had what they were owed. Gattie's warehouse would act in a similar way, with merchants transferring their outgoing goods to the warehouse, and collecting incoming goods for the way back. This would replace the need for thousands of carts to transfer items between each pair of merchants who had done business.

So far, so good. A very large facility for storing goods centrally would be impressive, but also immensely labour-intensive. Whilst individual merchants would avoid the need to sort and distribute many different loads, there would now be a greater risk of goods getting mixed up in the warehouse. Gattie foresaw this problem too, and applied electrical engineering to create a solution.

The result was the 'trucker': a motorized rail vehicle that would transport goods around the warehouse. The items would be placed onto metal trays upon arrival and the trays would be rolled onto the upper surface of the trucker. Electromechanical switches would be set that specified the destination for the item, and the trucker would move off along a loop of track in the warehouse. If it passed the bay for the chosen destination, upon arrival the tray would be rolled off, depositing the item in the correct location for its onward journey. However, given the size of the warehouse, most items would need to be transported by multiple truckers. The really clever part of the design was that different loops of rails would have their own truckers, with the loops arranged so that truckers on adjacent loops would pass closely. If an item needed to be moved from one loop to another, the truckers could slide them quickly and easily. Gattie even arranged a demonstration of this at his works, with the aid of the Irish playwright George Bernard Shaw. Shaw and Gattie had met previously, and despite his reservations about the technology, Shaw agreed to participate. He sat in an armchair with a glass of water at his feet, on top of a trucker that was set in motion along the tracks. He was swiftly transferred to another trucker travelling in the opposite direction, without a drop of water being spilt!

So why did this visionary scheme never happen? Timing was certainly a part of the problem, with the First World War taking place before Gattie had a chance to get the scheme underway. He continued to argue the case throughout the war, writing brusque letters to the Board of Trade (the Government department that would need to support the plans). A Bill was even deposited with Parliament in 1917.

Inside the warehouse, showing the railway sidings packed with wagons, lorries passing overhead on a bridge, and a gantry crane moving a container.

The main reason was the cost though. In 1910, Gattie estimated the cost of the warehouse at £6 million. By 1919, when the Board of Trade appointed a committee to examine the idea and make a decision, he suggested that the cost was now £12 million, and thought that total cost of implementing his scheme throughout the UK would be £300 million.

The committee also felt that Gattie has underestimated the congestion that would occur around the warehouse in London, and the cost of proposed additional railway connections that might be needed. The freight handling processes across London would also face a massive upheaval; together with all of the other considerations, the committee firmly rejected the plans.

A map showing how the freight warehouse would link to existing railways around the north of the City of London.

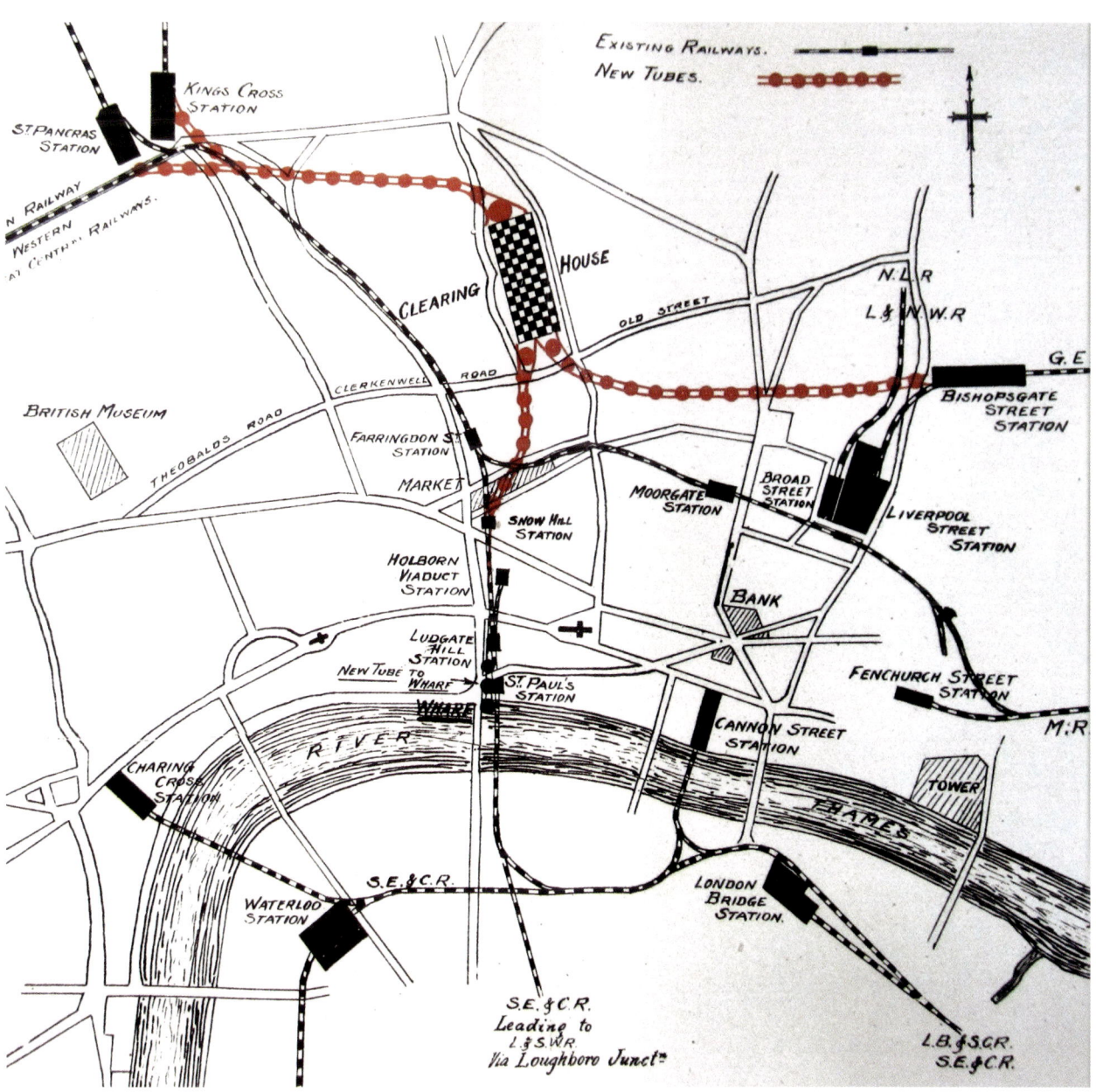

The Kearney Tubes

Elfric Wells Chalmers Kearney was an Australian inventor who spent most of his life promoting his schemes for a railway scheme that proposed placing one rail below and one rail above the carriages. This was eminently suitable for a tube railway, although it could also work on the surface through the use of pylons supporting the upper rail (like a heavier-duty version of a modern railway with an overhead electric wire).

His first plan for London, through the auspices of the Kearney High-Speed Railway Company, was produced in the first decade of the twentieth century. He publicized the scheme by building a model of the car and track in 1905, and then publishing a booklet in 1907. Two tube railway lines were proposed: one from Cricklewood to the Oval, and the second linking the Strand (in the vicinity of Temple station on the District Railway, and the now-closed Aldwych station on the Piccadilly Tube) with Crystal Palace, via Oval. Both lines would have a number of intermediate stations at key traffic centres for London.

One of the major innovations was that the stations would be built at surface level, or just below ground, with the tunnels dipping at 1 in 7 (just over 8°, or about twice as steep as a conventional railway) away from stations. The intention was that the cars would accelerate down the gradient up to a speed of around 60 mph, and then decelerate on their way up to the next station, needing only a small amount of additional energy to be provided from their electric motors. By building shallow stations, lifts would not be required, and those at surface level would be completely step-free. Each station would have a central departure platform between the two tracks, but would also have arrival platforms outside the tracks – this would allow passengers to alight onto the outside platforms as other passengers boarded, thus reducing the amount of stationary time required. The stations would also be designed to allow for the development of additional storeys above them, to provide further income.

Only a single tunnel would be constructed between each pair of stations, splitting into two tracks at the approach to the platforms. Points would be arranged so that as one train arrived at a station, another would be despatched into the freshly vacated tunnel in the opposite direction, maximizing the use of the tunnels and preventing a head-on collision.

The cars were designed with pointed ends to reduce air resistance through the tunnels. Drawings show single cars with both ends pointed, as well as end cars with a single pointed end which would run with one or more conventional cars in between. The end cars would seat 62 passengers; the intermediate and single cars 60 each. A paper written by Kearney in 1917 included a drawing of the interior of a car showing the pointed end and, amazingly to modern eyes, throw cushions on sumptuously upholstered seating, together with footstools.

Even if he failed as a railway promoter, Kearney was an excellent publicist. Over the years he had several working models constructed and put on display at prominent locations, such as the Olympia exhibition hall, the Crystal Palace, and a showroom on the Aldwych. The models were built to a generous scale of 6.25%, making a model car just over a metre long, and they coped with gradients of up to 1 in 3.

His plans for London went nowhere, either in 1907, or the following decade when he suggested a single single-track line linking North and South Woolwich, either side of the Thames. A similar scheme was then promoted in the 1930s, but this time linking North and South Shields in Tyneside. The River Tyne here is wide and shipping prevents construction of a bridge. He also suggested constructing the tunnels with integrated fold-down seating, allowing them to be quickly used as air-raid shelters. Despite petitioning many officials at all levels of local and central government (right up to Winston Churchill) no money was forthcoming and no tubes were built.

Kearney shows off one of his scale models of a single streamlined car. Stations were placed 90 feet apart, and Kearney estimated that the cars travelled at a scale speed of 400 mph!

The proposed interior of a High-Speed Railway car, showing the lounge at the pointed end. Public transport had never been so plush!

New roads for London: the early 1900s

London has proven, over the centuries, to be remarkably resilient to changes to its layout. New roads have occasionally been added, but these have never been on a scale that makes a substantial change to a wide area. Successful schemes included the New Road (now the Marylebone and Euston Roads), which formed the first bypass around the north side of the capital, and which was largely built through open land, and Kingsway, constructed at the start of the twentieth century as part of a slum clearance scheme between Holborn and the Strand.

Whilst Kingsway and Aldwych were being built, a Royal Commission on London Traffic was hearing evidence and considering what should be done to improve the traffic situation in London. Created partly as a result of almost wild speculation into tube railways at the turn of the century, the Commission's remit included roads. Its 1905 report recommended large-scale road widening to cope with the increasing volumes of traffic, together with the construction of two major new avenues crossing the capital.

The avenues were to be 140 ft wide, and run from Bayswater in the west, to Whitechapel, via Russell Square and the City, and from Holloway in the north to Elephant & Castle in the south, via Gray's Inn Road. Beneath both avenues, new railways would be built, and the width of the roads would allow for express and local tracks. The cutaway drawing that accompanied the report is very reminiscent of the New York subway, with platforms immediately below the street, and 'express' stations at which passengers could change between the express and local services. At street level, four lines of electric trams would also run. The similarity to New York was perhaps not a coincidence, given that the American city had opened its four-track subway just the year before.

As became usual with such schemes, the combination of cost, complexity of land acquisition, and general government inertia prevented the new roads from being built.

Given that motor cars were still only about a decade old, it seems amazing that Britain's first motorway was proposed between London and Brighton in 1902. This was to be a wide carriageway, carried above existing roads on bridges to avoid junctions, with separate lanes for fast and slow vehicles. The plan made is far as the House of Commons in 1906, as the London and Brighton Motor Way Bill, with a suggested price of just over £1·6 million. The plans showed it starting on the London Road between Norbury and Croydon, and then running south via Beddington, Chipstead, Redhill, and Haywards Heath to Patcham, just north of Brighton. The Bill was promoted in a very similar way to a railway Bill, but was withdrawn early on due to the level of opposition raised by landowners and railway companies.[9]

Another proposal for a motorway to Brighton was made in 1925, but with a route further west than the 1906 scheme. This would start on the new Kingston bypass (today's A3), and run via Epsom and Horsham to Albourne, again to the north of Brighton. Possible branches were shown to Southampton and Portsmouth, and to Worthing. The plans were put before Parliament in late 1928, but the following year failed due to lack of support. Surrey County Council in particular opposed the scheme, noting that there were already two main roads through the county on a similar route.[10]

An excerpt from a plan of the 1925 motorway scheme, showing the northern end from its divergence from the Kingston bypass and a tight curve near to Epsom.

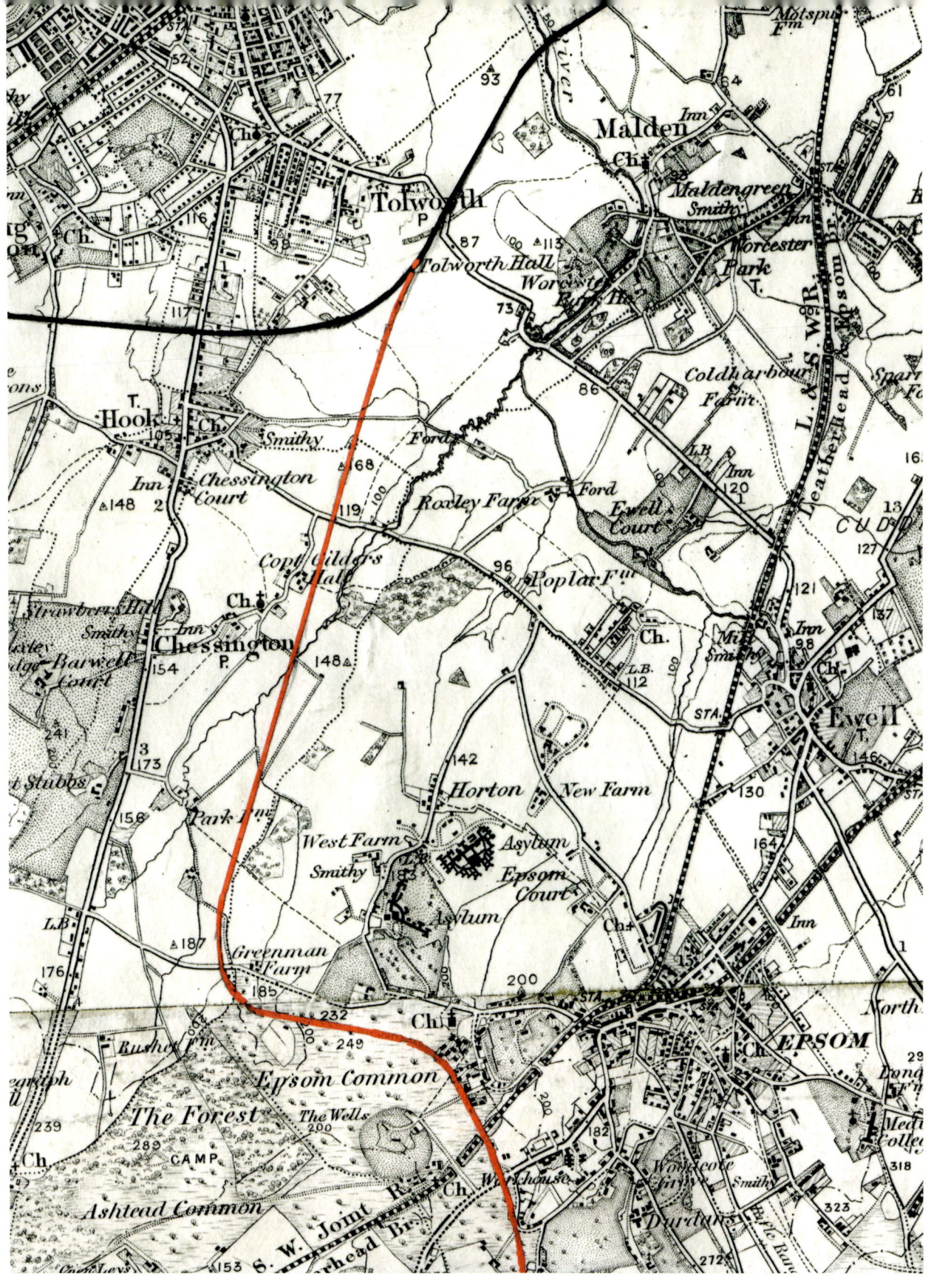

The Underground Goods Railway

Proposals for a tube railway to carry goods beneath London are not uncommon, but the greatest amount of publicity was probably obtained for the scheme in the 1920s. Originally put forward around 1925, the London Underground Goods Tube Railway appeared to be trying to cover all bases with its name, even though it had nothing to do with the passenger-carrying London Underground.

The plan was for 69 miles of tube railway linking the main-line station goods yards with each other, as well as the London docks and some of the wharves. At some, tunnels would rise to the surface as ramps; at others, huge electric lifts would be provided to raise and lower one or more wagons simultaneously. The sum of £32 million was going to be raised by both British and American banks to pay for the railway. The aim was to avoid the need to move goods around congested roads between the main-line stations, or via convoluted railway routes.

The railway was planning a series of radial lines converging on a huge underground depot that would allow trains to be split into separate wagons and reassembled for onward despatch. Originally this was to be at Leicester Square, but the promoters soon decided to buy the Foundling Hospital Estate in Bloomsbury instead. The tunnels would necessarily be able to accommodate main-line rolling stock, but electric locomotives would be used to move the wagons. The company hoped to persuade the main-line companies to sort the wagons into groups with a common destination, to minimize the shunting and rearrangement required at their depot; nonetheless, the goods company would need to provide a very large number of sidings for holding all the wagons. A report in late 1925 suggested that there would be up to 17,500 wagons on their system at any one time.[11]

It was even suggested that major shops in London would be able to receive goods directly from the railway, although this would have meant building additional tunnels in which trains could be stopped, together with lifts or conveyors to transfer the goods into the shop warehouses. An alternative was that tunnels would be built to connect the shops with the nearest station on the system; this was a better solution as it would avoid the need for trains to stop frequently in closely spaced stations.

A map was produced, showing how the tunnels would stretch from Hammersmith in the west across to the Bishopsgate Goods Yard in the east, with branches to Battersea and Bricklayers Arms. To the north, connections would link to and from the goods yards at Paddington, Marylebone, Camden, St Pancras, and King's Cross. A complex, and somewhat confusing tangle of tunnels under Soho would link the four radial arms of the scheme together; no explanation of why so many tunnels were planned has been found, nor why these were beneath Soho rather than being at the Foundling Hospital site, although it would seem that the plans had changed by this point to remove the need for a vast central depot and instead have many smaller stations around the network, each with their own sidings, storage, and connections to the surface. These would use chutes for goods transferring to the railway, and conveyors to take goods from the railways to surface buildings, which would include neighbouring department stores.

A Committee was appointed to report on the plan, comprising representatives from each of the four main-line railway groups, via their regular General Managers' Conference, which was chaired by Robert Selbie (General Manager of the Metropolitan Railway). The members were not convinced that the tube would pay its way. They noted in their report at the end of 1925 that the main-line companies had already built facilities to exchange goods between their railways, mostly away from the centre of London, and would be reluctant to abandon these. The additional clerical work in documenting the movement of goods onto and away from the tube railway would be considerable, and it was not clear how they would make sufficient money to pay for this, let alone show a return on the original investment.

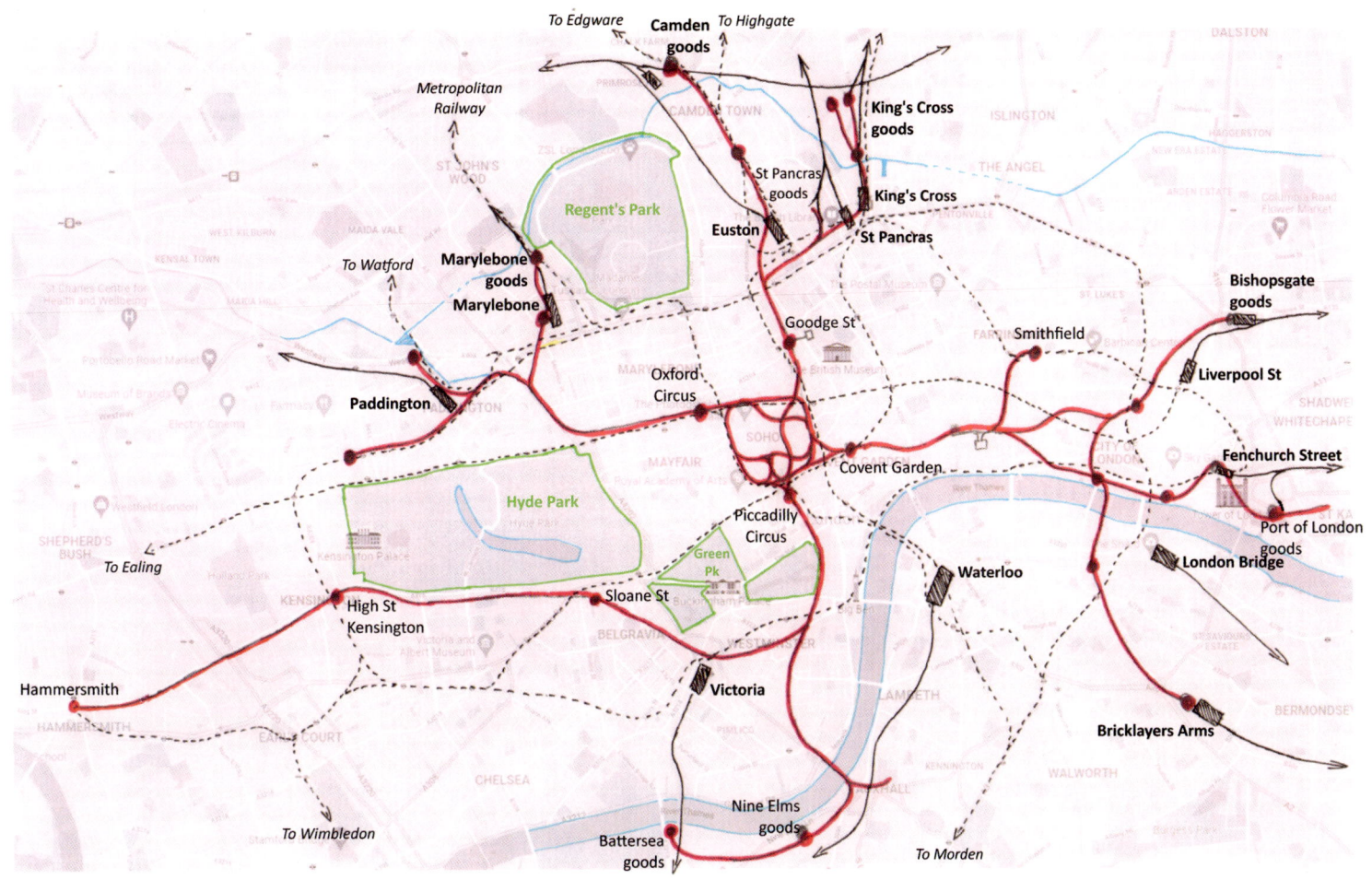

The unusual layout of the planned railway tunnels in 1925, superimposed on a modern map of London and also showing the route of the Underground lines in operation at the time.

Bar the occasional press report, nothing much happened with the underground goods railway plan, other than the cost increasing. At the beginning of 1927 a new group of promoters acquired the rights to the scheme and started to revive the plans. The immediately paid a visit to Selbie to ask if he would be able to arrange for the revised plans to be reconsidered.

The new plans were dramatically reduced in scope from before. Some 20 miles of tunnel were now planned, containing narrow-gauge tracks, at a cost of around £5 million. Five goods depots would be provided, together with connections into a number of major shops, hotels, and markets. The goods to be handled by the railway included:

- Shop and warehouse goods
- Meat for Central Markets
- Shipping traffic for London, St Katharine Docks, and adjacent wharves
- Small parcels "Passenger Train Traffic"
- Mails
- Coal for internal delivery only.

The list shows a certain naïvety on the part of the promoters in understanding the existing freight flows around London. Meat for the Central Markets at Smithfield was already brought by rail into the basement of the market buildings, through a connection from the Metropolitan Railway's City Widened Lines. This seems to have been recognized by August 1927, when the promoters dropped this idea. Mails were on the cusp of being transferred beneath London by the Post Office's own underground railway, which had been constructed, delayed by World War One, and was due to open in 1927. The Post Office would not have been keen to see its investment reduced in value by another company attempting to take over its traffic. Coal is a messy product, and unless completely separate facilities for handling it were provided at additional cost (including substantial storage facilities) it would rapidly have contaminated the rest of the system.

Although a map was supplied, the promoters made it clear to the Conference that they wanted to be advised as to suitable routes, tunnel sizes, and the types of good that they should carry. The railway managers were not happy at this request, feeling that if they provided such advice then they would be tacitly approving the scheme.[12] They instead decided to ask the promoters to put forward a definite proposal on which comment could be made.

This plan appears to have come to nothing, and within two years the original scheme was being resurrected. A short report in *The Times* in 1929 noted the cost as now being £40 million. Tapping into the general concern about unemployment, the promoters noted that construction would occupy 60,000 men for four years. The scheme was "being considered" by the Minister for Employment, having been sponsored by Viscount Elibank, who was one of the promoters. Again, after a flurry of discussions everything went quiet.

In 1932, a new proposal on rather familiar lines hit the newspapers following an inaugural dinner. The Goodsway was a reheated version of the previous scheme, with a new company name and a different list of promoters, with the exception of its chairman, Cedric Erlund, who seems to be a common figure linking all of the schemes apart from the 1927 narrow-gauge plan.

The cost had now risen to £45 million, but despite this, the promoters confidently claimed to be able to start work "within the next few months".[13] Eighty miles of track would connect 55 goods stations, with links to all the main-line railways and the Underground. The tracks would be in tunnels 16 feet in diameter and would be electrified using third rails. Each station tunnel would be placed on a loop to the side of the running tunnel, allowing trains that did not need to stop at the station to pass by non-stop.

Although the tunnels would be large enough for main-line trains to use, such trains would only be permitted to use the system to run from one company's network to another. The tunnel stations would be too small to permit the loading and unloading of main-line wagons, and so goods intended for destinations in London would need to be handled in special smaller wagons. These would be automatically operated, and individually motorized, allowing them to operate singly rather than needing trains to be assembled. Presumably the success of a similar system on the recently opened Post Office Railway had inspired the promoters.

All goods on the system would be placed into standardized containers, 5×4×3 feet, intended for a single destination. These would be taken to the loading station on conveyors or by a fleet of vans, and would be grouped by destination. The next wagon passing through the station for the same destination, and with available capacity, would collect the containers and take them on their way.

Twenty-two of the stations would also have coal depots, consisting of 60,000-ton bunkers. Main-line coal wagons would be brought through the tunnels, and the wagons lifted and emptied using wagon lifts.

The new scheme was again put to the General Railway Managers' Conference, who wrote back to Erlund on 2 March 1932. They considered that the scheme would involve considerable transhipment of goods between different wagons, increasing the costs and making the proposal infeasible. The proposals for coal did not address how different grades and quality of coal would be handles, nor how ownership would be managed. The Conference declined to offer any further encouragement, and from this point the scheme disappears from the record.

A map of the rather smaller 1927 proposals, with the tunnels in red and the five 'Distribution Stations' in green. The smaller red blobs show key buildings that the promoters thought might be interested in connecting to the system, including Selfridge's (1), the Army & Navy Stores (10), the Piccadilly Hotel (14) and Covent Garden Market (27). Somewhat later, the Greater London Council examined the idea of building an underground goods railway in the early 1970s. They concluded that the £100 million scheme, with around 17 depots, would only reduce the traffic levels in London by five percent, and would slow down the distribution of goods because of the need to transfer them onto the new system.[14]

King's Cross airport

The 1920s saw air travel start to make the transition from an experimental mode of transport into something a little more mainstream. It was seen as being futuristic, and an Underground poster of 1926 depicted the skies above London filled with aircraft in a century.[15] It was probably not surprising then that suggestions were made for airports closer to central London than the existing airport at Croydon, opened in 1920 as London's main facility, and the brochure issued for the King's Cross airport noted that the need to travel between London and Croydon added forty minutes to the journey.

The architect Charles Glover proposed a new airport in 1931, to be located just north of the main-line stations at King's Cross and St Pancras. The land here was dominated by railways: sidings, goods sheds, and facilities for servicing locomotives and carriages. But these were essential to the railway companies, and could not be cleared for an airport. Glover's idea was to put the airport above the railway.

He proposed a circular airport, half-a-mile in diameter, with four 200-ft-wide runways crossing at a central point and surrounded by a circular taxiway. This remarkable concrete structure would sit on the top of a series of new buildings 120 ft high. Some of these would act as multi-storey hangars for the aircraft, with lifts taking them to runway level – bear in mind that aircraft were far smaller in those days than the huge planes that are in use today. The passenger terminal building would also provide access via lifts. Once ready to go, the aircraft would taxi around the edge to the correct runway before taking off. The choice of runway would be determined by the wind direction, and lighting would ensure that only the correct runway would be used (controlled automatically by a weathervane). Above the airport, a beacon light would allegedly be visible to an aircraft over Paris![16]

Some of the buildings beneath the airport would act as cargo warehouses for goods arriving and departing by air. Railway sidings passing through the buildings at ground level would make it easy to switch good from one more of transport to another. The possibility of transferring good onto barges using the Grand Union Canal was also considered, as the canal would pass through the site next to the southern edge of the airport area.

The area north of the stations and east of York Road was, for much of the nineteenth and twentieth centuries, poor-quality housing for the working classes, bordering on slums in places, and so there was a 'social improvement' element to the project. Many of these houses would be cleared to construct a large market facility, and replacement housing in tenement blocks would be built for the people whose existing houses would be demolished.

The centre crossing point would be supported by four buildings, with larger towers beneath the taxiway where each runway joined. Another tower would support the taxiway between each of the runway connections, and the runways themselves would have two towers between the taxiway and the crossing point – in total, 36 towers.

The passenger terminal building was to be at the south-eastern corner of the airport, immediately north of the Regent's Canal and east of York Road. It would be approached via Aerial Way, a new road that would push in a southeasterly direction through the existing street pattern to a junction with the Caledonian Road. These buildings would include a large coach and bus station (capable of handling 150 vehicles) to provide connections for onward travel. Escalators would descend to the Underground – presumably the Piccadilly line at York Road station, which would have been a little to the north of the terminal building.

In June 1931 a model of the proposal was put on show at Charing Cross Underground station, and then at the Institution of Civil Engineers. In 1933, the model was shown at the Oil Industries Exhibition, and a company was formed to promote the airport – Central Airports Ltd, and Glover was one of its Directors. The exhibitions, together

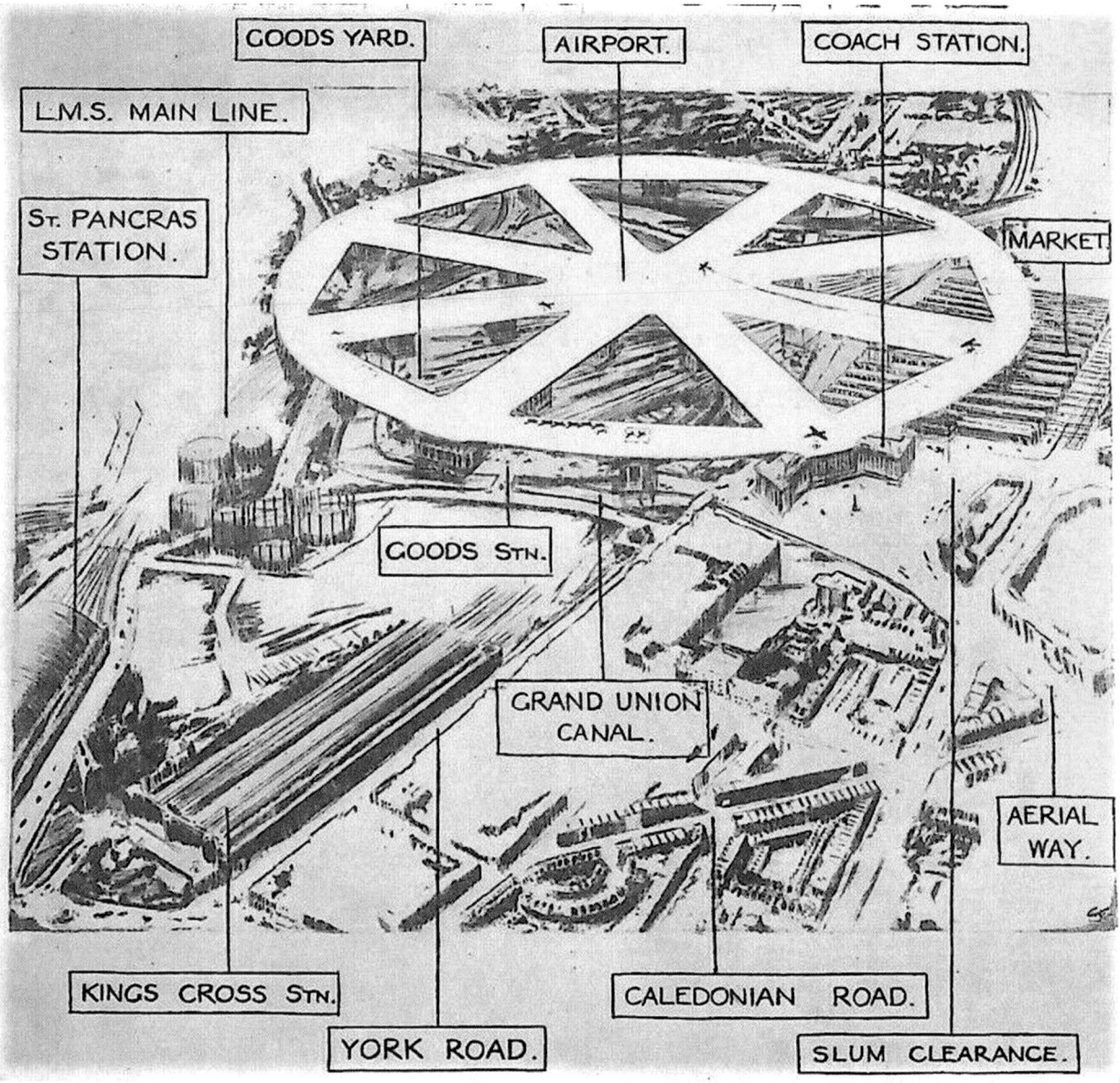

with articles in newspapers and magazines all helped with publicity, and apparently support was forthcoming from businessmen who fancied keeping a plane near the City, but no further progress was made.

The idea had many drawbacks, aside from the estimated cost of £5 million and the logistics of having to build 36 tower blocks across an active railway site. There was no safe run-off zone if a plane overshot a runway or was blown sideways at take-off or landing. The airport could not be expanded for larger planes, which would probably have limited its active life to twenty years at most, despite the view of the promotors that improvements in wheel-brakes "and other landing and taking-off devices" would allow for runways to be made even shorter. Had it been built, it would have made a magnificent target for German bombers in the Second World War. It would also have impeded the building of skyscrapers in London from the 1960s. Ultimately, it was an idea that was never going to take off.

The Charing Cross Bridge

For much of its life, the railway bridge into Charing Cross station has been the subject of plans to demolish it. Why should the centre of London, and the views along the Thames, be spoiled by an ugly metal railway bridge? Indeed, *Punch* magazine published a cartoon in 1923 in which the 'Spirit of Ugliness' declared the bridge to be his masterpiece! And yet the bridge remains, masked slightly since 2012 by the pair of footbridges constructed either side to mark the Queen's Golden Jubilee. Ironically, many of the plans involved replacing the bridge by a road bridge.

One of the first of these was in 1908, when Thomas Collcutt, the architect of the Palace Theatre and the Savoy Hotel, proposed a bridge lined with shops connecting to the Embankment on the north side, with a circular plaza.

A drawing of the Waterhouse scheme from 1924, looking south-east across the new bridge towards the south bank.

In 1916, when one might have thought that there were more pressing priorities, *The Sphere* published a plan for the removal of Charing Cross station and its bridge.[17] The station would be relocated onto the South Bank, immediately west of the approach to Waterloo Bridge, on the site of the Lion Brewery (and now the site of the Royal Festival and Queen Elizabeth Halls). Its east side would be bounded by a new approach road to the new Charing Cross road bridge. A low-level embankment path would remain for pedestrians along the riverside, with a higher-level pathway linking the bridges at road level. Beneath the station service roads would provide access for deliveries.

Despite the war raging in Europe, Charing Cross seemed to be a pressing problem. The following year, the architect William Caröe published plans for Waterloo East station to be rebuilt and enlarged as a major terminus that would face Waterloo across a new plaza. Charing Cross and its bridge would be removed, and a five-arched stone road bridge would span the Thames, on a slightly different alignment. This was to be named the Bridge of Empire.

Other proposals around the same time located the station in either a similar place, or terminating directly on the riverbank. Some focused purely on the replacement of the railway bridge and station, whilst others included wider replanning: for example, Paul Waterhouse's plan of 1924 would have seen widespread reconstruction of the whole of the Southbank and Southwark areas.

A Royal Commission on Cross-River Traffic reported in 1926, and recommended a new bridge at Charing Cross, as well as widening John Rennie's much-loved Waterloo Bridge, despite the fact that the latter was suffering serious structural problems. Subsidence towards its north end had necessitated the construction of a temporary bridge alongside in 1925, to take some of the traffic.

It was 1929 when the London County Council (LCC) officially decided to support plans for the Charing Cross Bridge. Their Chief Engineer, Sir

A model of the LCC approved scheme, showing the replacement station in white, with ridge-and-furrow roof at upper centre, with Waterloo below and to the right. On the other side of the Thames are new buildings and roads.

George Humphrys, prepared plans for a double-deck bridge that would link the upper road level to the north bank at the level of the Strand. Crossing the site of the former station, the road would terminate on the Strand at a large square plaza, which models of the time suggested would be surrounded by a set of matching buildings.[18]

As with the 1916 proposal described above, the station at Charing Cross would be relocated onto the South Bank on the Lion Brewery site, with the agreement of the Southern Railway company, which owned the station. The roads that crossed the site, as well as the spaces between the new station and the existing Waterloo station, would be placed into large tunnels beneath the elevated tracks.

A plan of the approved scheme, showing how the new road network would connect with existing roads and loop around the stations.

The LCC submitted the London County Council (Charing Cross Bridge) Bill to the 1930 session of Parliament. It was rejected by a Select Committee of the House of Commons, which objected to proposed site for the replacement station on the south bank.

The Bill was resubmitted in 1931, with the understanding that the scheme would cost no more than £12·5 million, and that the Government would cover 75% of the cost. However, Britain's worsening economic situation forced this offer to be rescinded – due in part to concerns that Waterloo Bridge would require complete replacement. With the prospect of no Government funding, the 1931 Bill also failed. A 60% grant towards the rebuilding of Waterloo Bridge was offered by the Government in January 1932, and the following month this was accepted by the LCC.[19]

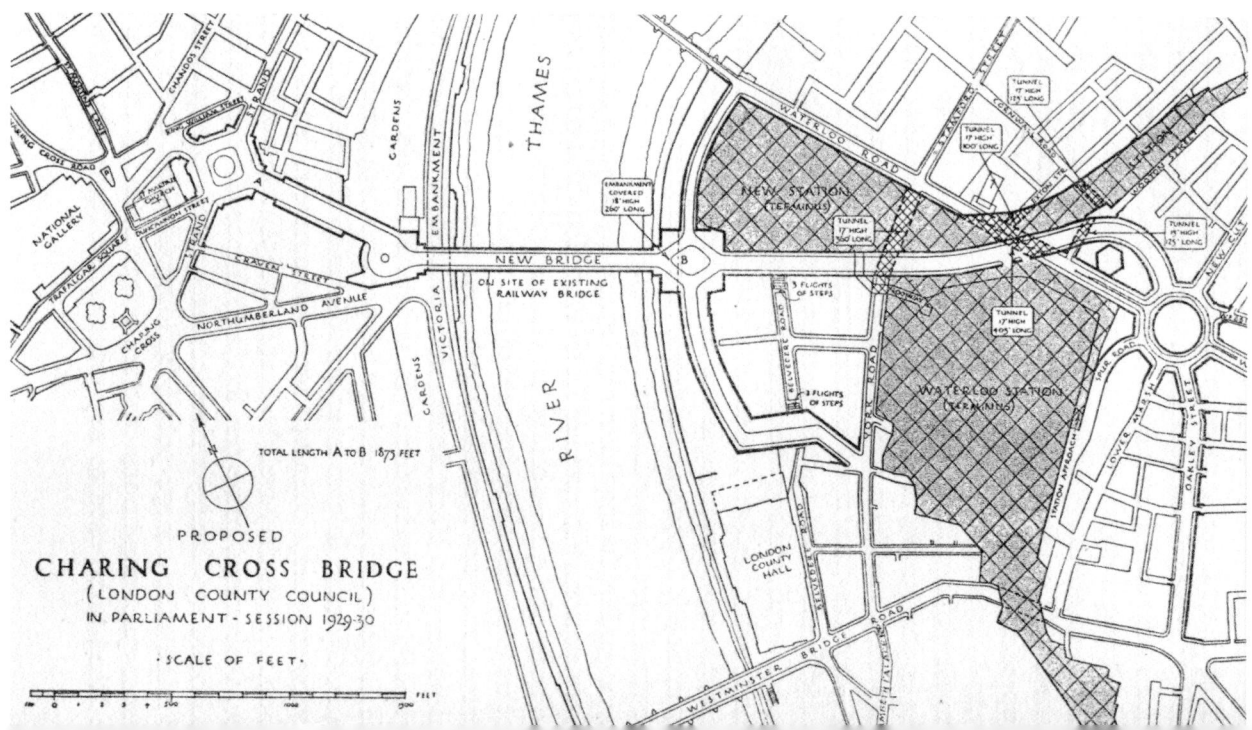

Peckham Thames

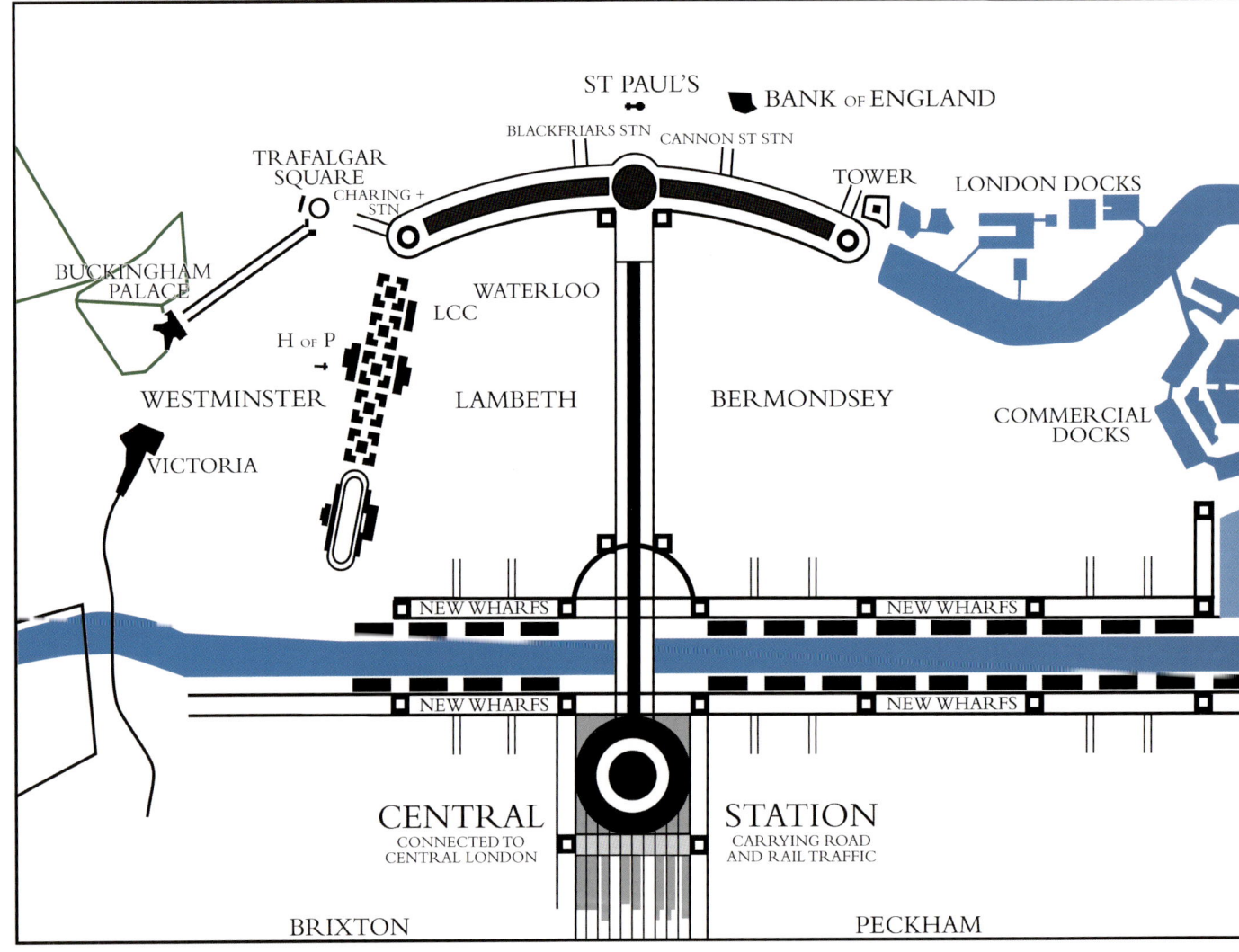

In 1933 the architect and draughtsman William Walcot proposed a plan to reroute the Thames through Peckham, leaving just a short stub to serve the Pool of London and St Katherine Docks at the far end, together with the Surrey Docks on the south side. The rest of the Thames between Tower Bridge and Vauxhall would become a wide boulevard (to Westminster) and then a set of gardens south to Vauxhall, where the new channel would rejoin the original course of the river upstream. The boulevard would have a large roundabout at each end – Charing Cross and Tower Bridge – and an even larger one at the centre point, to the south of St Paul's Cathedral.

As it headed eastward, the new channel would roughly follow the course of the existing Grand Surrey Canal, with a new harbour taking up much of Deptford. The channel would link back to its original course at the south end of the Isle of Dogs. The Greenwich Peninsula, site of the Millennium Dome (now the O_2) would be made into an island by a new channel to the south, straightening out the curve between Greenwich and Woolwich. A seaplane base was suggested as a suitable use.

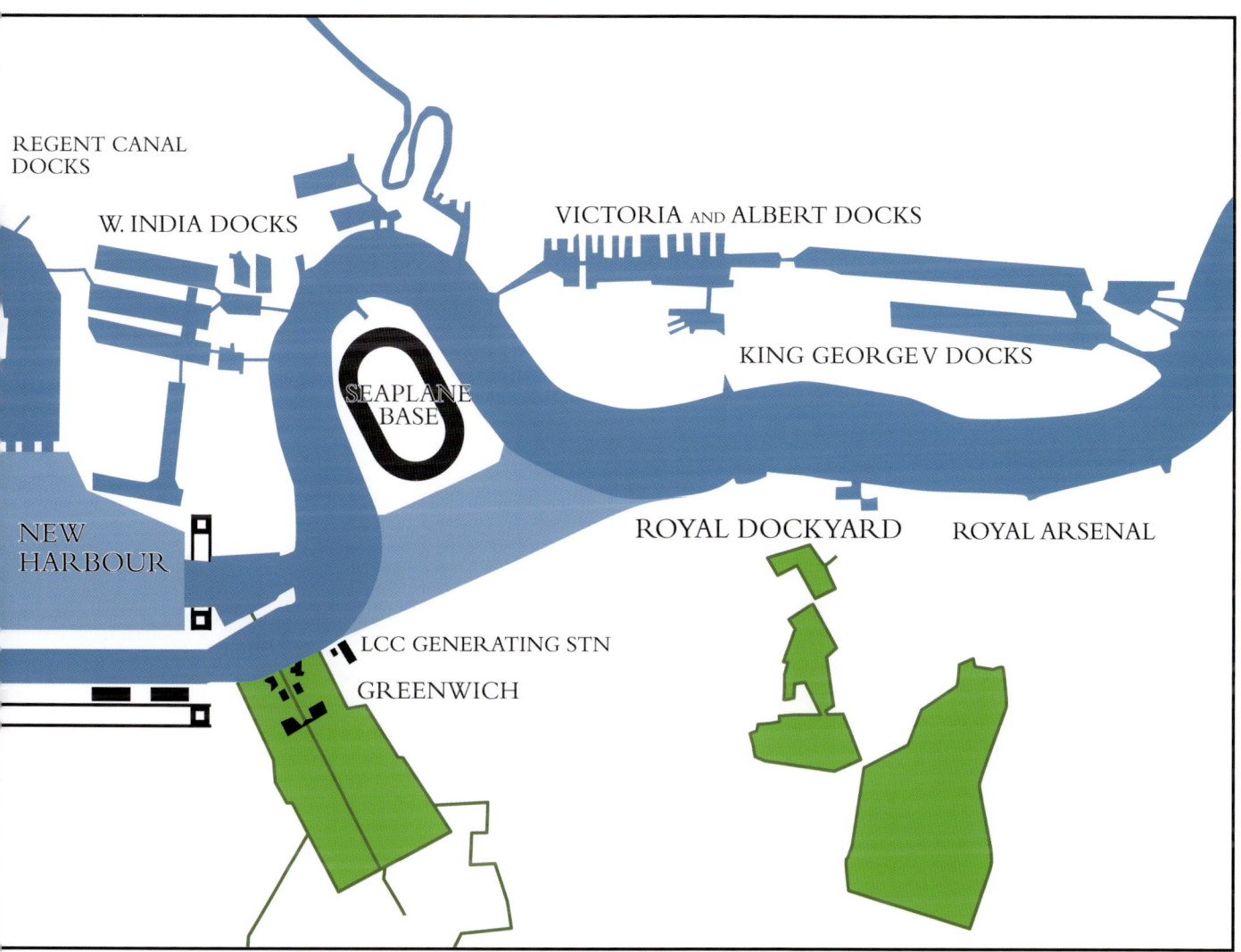

A new major station would be built at Kennington to replace those at Waterloo, Victoria, and London Bridge. The station was to have an airport above it. A road and rail link would run due north to speed passengers into central London.

The work was estimated to cost a staggering £500 million, although with the amount of land that the new river channel, station and road/rail link would require, the digging of the river, and the fact that the land along the original river course would not be sold (since it was for roads and gardens) this is probably a considerable underestimate

This map is based on a similar map published at the time Walcot proposed his ambitious plan.

The "Tideless Thames" barrage

In 1944, the Thames Barrage Association (TBA) published a book entitled "Tideless Thames in Future London". This set out, though a series of essays, the argument for constructing a dam across the Thames to the east of London, allowing the water to be retained at mean high tide level through the capital. This, it was claimed, would bring about a number of benefits.

The Thames today is divided into tidal and non-tidal sections, the two meeting at Teddington lock. This division was defined in 1908 when the Port of London Authority was created, with responsibility for the tidal section. The tides between Teddington and the river mouth have always complicated the use of the river; they make it harder for shipping that wishes to travel against the flow, and the wharfs that used to exist upstream of London Bridge were only accessible at high tide. Sewage poured into the river east of London had to be timed to coincide with the ebb tide, to avoid being washed back upstream, hence the provision of large storage tanks at the sewage works at Beckton and Crossness.

A barrage would help to solve all of these problems, and more, according to the TBA. Fires near the foreshore could not be easily extinguished at low tide as the river water could not easily be accessed. In spring, the fickle tides could rise higher than usual, and flood large areas of the low-lying land to the east of the City of London. The TBA produced a list of twenty such benefits, which also included the possibility of providing an airport for seaplanes along a stretch of river at Chelsea Reach, which would only be possible with a consistent water level.

The suggestion of a barrage across the Thames goes back into Victorian times. Before London Bridge was rebuilt by John Rennie in 1831, its 19 narrow and irregularly spaced arches (four of which were occupied by waterwheels) formed a partial dam and caused the water to be up to 2 metres higher on the upstream side, which was also wider and slower-flowing than today because of the lack of the Thames embankments, built in the 1860s. This was one of the reasons that the river occasionally froze over, giving rise to the famous "Frost Fairs". Rennie's new bridge led to a faster flow, and in 1858 a suggestion was made to build a dam alongside the bridge. The sewage pouring into the Thames at the time prevented this from being a practical proposition, as it would have turned the river through London into a foetid cesspool (well, even more so than it already was).

A Thames Barrage Committee was established in the early twentieth century, and proposed damming the river at Gravesend. At this point the barrage would have to be 2,400 feet wide, and would have at its mid-point six locks of different sizes to allow vessels to pass from one side to the other. Sluice gates between the locks and the shorelines would allow the flow of water to be carefully controlled. The structure would also incorporate road and rail tunnels in its foundations to provide additional cross-river connections.[20]

The Port of London Authority ignored the proposal, much to the disgust of the later TBA. Another proposal was made in 1928 by Lord Desborough, the former chairman of the Thames Conservancy Board. This followed a flood that killed 14 people in London at the start of the year, caused by a combination of a high tide, storms in the North Sea, and heavy rainfall in the Thames region. Newspapers at the time published drawings of the proposed barrages, but again, nothing happened.

The TBA, formed in 1935, aimed to build on the work of the earlier Committee, and raised funds and awareness of their project. Their proposal was for the barrage to be located at Woolwich, a short distance downstream from the modern Thames Flood Barrier. In other respects it was to be very similar to the Gravesend barrage, with six locks and a rail tunnel beneath; the major difference was that a roadway connecting the North and South Circular Roads was to be carried on a bridge over the upstream ends of the locks.

The Association was ready for a planned public inquiry being arranged by the Government in 1938. A legal team had been assembled; documents prepared; models built. The Minister of Transport then cancelled the inquiry less than 24 hours before it was due to start because of the worsening political situation in Europe. Concerns were voiced about the barrage being an attractive target for bombing in the event of war.

Undeterred, the promoters adjusted their scheme. Their new plan was for the main barrage to span the Thames at Galleons Reach, with vessels using a 500 ft long ship canal excavated parallel to the river on its south side. This would be easier to construct in stages, and would require a simpler bridge for the roadway crossing. It was too late though, as the Second World War would put off all engineering projects not necessary for winning. By 1944, the tide was turning though, and an end to the conflict appeared in sight. The TBA published their book and plans in the hope that the project could be carried out once peace was declared. Like so many ideas of the age, it was frustrated by the lack of money: Britain had to concentrate on rebuilding its damaged infrastructure, and could not afford any grandiose plans.

The 1935 scheme at Woolwich, which was rejected by the Government, included six adjacent locks, each with a double-deck bascule bridge at the west end carrying a road on the upper level and a railway beneath.

Revitalizing the South Bank

By the end of the 1940s, Britain was placing the horrors of the Second World War behind it, and the Government felt that the time was right for a national celebration. The Festival of Britain was planned for 1951, one century on from the Great Exhibition that saw the construction of the Crystal Palace in Hyde Park; this centenary had sparked the first idea for the Festival, back in 1943. A site on the south bank of the Thames was chosen for London's part of the event: bombed in the war, it was derelict and in need of complete reconstruction.

The main structures that were provided for the Festival have been well-documented: the Dome of Discovery, the Skylon, and the Royal Festival Hall. However, in 1946 the designer Misha Black had proposed an incredible glass building that would have covered much of the site. A roadway would spiral around the outside, forming a long ramp rising to the roof level. Buildings within the spiral would be clad in curved glass, giving the whole structure a single shape. At the top, a pylon would allow visitors to ascend to a viewing platform 1,500 feet above London. Although his illustration showed the buildings on the south bank site, Black noted that "it could be positioned equally well in Hyde Park or Regent's Park".[21]

Following the end of the Festival of Britain, the site remained largely clear. From the northern side of County Hall, all the way round to Waterloo Bridge, the only building was the new Royal Festival Hall, together with a few older structures. A decade after the Festival finished, a proposal was made to create a new destination in London: South Bank New Town.[22] Noting that the southern side of the river had, for centuries, been London's pleasure ground, with sites ranging from the bear pit, through The Globe theatre, to the Festival itself, it was felt that the site could now provide an alternative to London's West End. The area had few buildings of architectural merit, and could be redeveloped more cheaply than the West End.

Transport connections would be provided via Waterloo station, which already had pedestrian links through to the riverside, and would become "a giant transport interchange". Visitors would be attracted by "sky signs" (presumably illuminated advertising like at Piccadilly Circus) visible from across the river, and the attractions, including "theatres, dance halls, exhibitions, restaurants, bowling alleys, pubs, sports arenas, pleasure gardens, bandstands, the lot". Offices and flats would be provided in a series of tower buildings, with the tallest of these built over Waterloo station, and reducing in height towards the river. It was felt that these would help to "neutralise" the effect of the Shell Centre tower, described as looking like "some giant's wardrobe dumped down on Thameside". Buildings would be projected out over the riverside walkway to provide shelter to pedestrians.

Key to making the plan a success was the link to the north bank. The existing Hungerford footbridge was a narrow, dreary walkway alongside Charing Cross Railway Bridge (replaced in 2002 by the Golden Jubilee Bridges). This would not provide the experience desired by the planners, nor have sufficient capacity for the number of people that they hoped would want to walk over the river. Instead, the plans included a radical idea for the railway bridge.

The preferred approach was to close Charing Cross station completely, and resite it on the south side of the river. The bridge, dubbed the "Live Link", would then be rebuilt with shops along the centre line, and a broad walkway either side, incorporating moving walkways to speed people across the bridge. Above the shops would be restaurants.

A modern rendering of Misha Black's improbable 1946 glass structure, which would have dominated the area for miles around.

Top: The New Town scheme included a suggestion for a new leisure harbour on the South Bank. Bottom: How Charing Cross Bridge might look if closed to trains and repurposed as a leisure venue.

If the station could not be moved then a new deck would be built above the railway carrying the shops and walkways. This would not be able to incorporate the extra restaurant level, or the moving walkways. Either way, the bridge would become an extension of the South Bank area, linking across to the shops at the Strand, and helping to unclog areas such as the West End around Leicester Square, which was felt to be too small for the numbers visiting.[23]

Top: A view of the South Bank from across the river, with Waterloo Bridge on the right, showing the appearance of the South Bank New Town scheme.
Bottom: How Charing Cross Bridge and the South Bank would look from the river.

Further transport links would be provided at the South Bank through new jetties for leisure boats. A small harbour might also be formed by indenting the river bank and dredging (to avoid the harbour becoming a muddy area at low tide). Illustrations show steps leading down to the water's edge.

As with so many grandiose planning schemes for London, this came to nothing. A new National Theatre was built on the eastern side of Waterloo Bridge, but this was already in the planning stages when the New Town was proposed. Together with the Royal Festival Hall and Hayward Gallery, with their linking structures, this now forms one of London's most distinctive and well-known brutalist set of buildings.

A disadvantage of the South Bank complex is the open-air nature of the connections, exposing pedestrians to the weather. In the 1990s, a competition was held to reinvigorate the locality, which was won by the architectural practice of Richard Rogers. Their proposal was for an undulating glass roof to be constructed over the whole area: this would shield people from the elements, particularly on the windswept upper concourses. The curving shape would be distinctive, and also assist with air flows, helping to provide natural ventilation.

Beneath the new canopy, significant work would take place to improve the public areas, by creating new performance spaces and facilities such as cafés and restaurants, and improving the connectivity of the buildings across the site, as well as to nearby transport hubs such as Waterloo and the Charing Cross bridge. The Hungerford footbridge would be reconstructed as well. Over £10 million was raised towards the initial estimated £70 million cost. By 1997 the estimate had risen to £130 million, with around £50 million allocated by the National Lottery,[24] but the Arts Council failed to agree on its overall strategy for the area and the project fell through. Individual buildings in the Southbank complex were subsequently renovated, and most recently the adjacent Shell Centre has undergone substantial redevelopment.

The Charing Cross heliport

Passengers arriving at Charing Cross station could have had a wider range of destinations if the heliport proposed in 1951 had come to fruition. The plans were aired at the end of the year, with accompanying drawings showing a large elevated platform extending out over the river Thames at roof height. This would have a 300-ft-diameter circular landing area, with lifts either side to lower helicopters to a storage deck – in effect, helicopter parking – just beneath. Passengers would access the helicopters from arrival and departure buildings on the north-west side of the platform that would connect into the large terminal building to be constructed above the platforms of Charing Cross station.

The building would contain all the necessary facilities for an international airport, including police and customs, as well as air traffic control. Lifts would move passengers between levels, providing an effective interchange between (from top to bottom) the heliport, main-line trains, road vehicles on the Victoria Embankment, the District line, and finally the Northern and Bakerloo lines, deep below in tube tunnels.

The landing area would be formed of reinforced concrete, 70 ft above ground level, with slender concrete columns placed in the Thames and the gardens either side of the station.

The plans were drawn up by the London firm of Asland and Freeman, who were architects and town planners, at the request of the MP Norman Dodds.[25] He felt that the advent of the twin-engined helicopter meant that it would be safe to fly directly over urban areas. The heliport would provide direct flights within the UK and internationally, as well as providing connecting services to London Airport (Heathrow) and Northolt aerodrome. Safety would be increased by directing the helicopters along the route of the river, rather than directly over central London.

The plan was considered cautiously, and the following year had been modified to raise the platform to a height of 100 ft above ground level, and making it 300 ft square. This would accommodate two runways 300 ft long and 150 ft wide, complying with the Inter-Departmental Helicopter Committee requirements.[26]

There appears to have been no progress with the idea until in June 1954 the Government authorized British European Airways to purchase two Sikorsky S55 helicopters, fitted with floats. These operated scheduled passenger services to Heathrow airport from the Waterloo Air Terminal, next to County Hall, which reused one of the Festival of Britain buildings. It wasn't a commercial success, closing down in 1956.

The Times reported that "the Government could not contemplate the considerable expenditure which must be involved in the construction of a permanent air stop for London".[27] They wanted to know that the market for helicopter flights existed before committing a large sum of money to building a heliport. As part of the BEA trial, the Government had agreed to allow any helicopters to operate over much of central London without permission, so long as they stayed above 1,000 ft (except during take-off and landing).

Although unbuilt, the proposal might have been one of the triggers for the Ministry of Aviation to appoint a panel of experts in the late 1950s to examine possible sites for a central London heliport. By the time their report was published in 1961, a temporary facility had been opened in Battersea, partially over the Thames. This remains London's most central heliport today. However, noise and cost were major factors preventing the large-scale introduction of commercial helicopter flights from central London, together with safety concerns. In 2013 the tragic accident at St George's Wharf Tower in Vauxhall demonstrated the risks of flights over a city that was building more and more skyscrapers.[28]

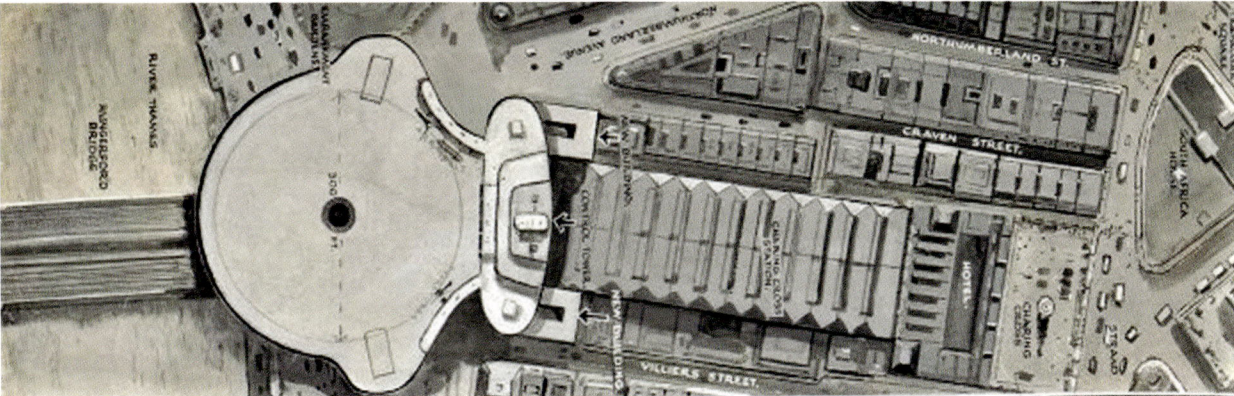

Drawings of the heliport scheme, giving a sense of scale, together with a cross-section (top right) showing how the existing railways, roads, and Underground lines would remain beneath. The aerial view gives a feel for just how much of an area would be rendered in shadow to the south of Charing Cross station.

High Paddington

The goods yard to the north of Paddington station once occupied an area of around 18 acres. The space is now taken up by a series of office buildings, together with the Westway elevated road, but in the early 1950s it was proposed for a new town 100ft above the ground.

The High Paddington plan of 1952 looked to take the block bounded by the Harrow Road, Warwick Avenue, Bishop's Bridge Road, and Westbourne Bridge, and construct a town for 8,000 people above the railway. The goods yard would remain, but completely covered over by a concrete deck. A facility for handling deliveries by road would be above this, with car parks, light industry, and facilities such as a swimming pool further up the building. This would cover the entire site to a height of 100 ft, forming the basic podium for the scheme. A centralized heating system would provide warmth to all of the apartments, offices, and other facilities in the development.

This level would form the base for the new town. A central piazza, suitable for holding exhibitions and events, would have three tower blocks around it, containing the apartments. The highest block would be topped by a new church "rising above the other buildings in the honoured tradition of our villages, towns, and great cities". The apartments would be on two levels, and would each have their own private gardens, large enough to grow flower, shrubs, and even small trees. The gardens would be placed behind perforated glazing, providing shelter from bad weather but allowing light and air. This would also help to keep the houses warmer in the winter (by providing extra insulation) and allow them to be cooled by breezes in the summer. There would also be communal gardens and playgrounds around the edge of the main podium.

The ground floors of these blocks would contain the shops and other communal facilities, and a primary school would be at the top of one of the buildings. The third tower would be topped by roof gardens, restaurants, and a television studio, with a small hospital on the floors immediately beneath.

A series of lifts and corridors would ensure that everywhere was easy to access, and no apartment would be more than a few minutes away from the podium-level facilities. Paddington station would be just across Bishop's Bridge Road, with the Underground station (on today's Circle and Hammersmith & City lines) being especially close.

Additional open space would be made at ground level around High Paddington by covering over the railway tracks east of Royal Oak station and Lord Hill's Bridge to create playing fields for the school. These would be joined directly to Westbourne Green, as the Westway had not yet been planned. Illustrations prepared for the plan suggest that the blocks of houses between Gloucester Terrace and Westbourne Terrace would also be cleared to form open space running southwards towards Hyde Park. Only the Holy Trinity church would have remained, ironically given that this was demolished in 1984, having been closed in 1971 after the building was found to be unsafe. Part of the aim was to provide green space for the inhabitants of High Paddington by removing old, derelict buildings.[29]

A cutaway drawing of a proposed apartment, showing the gardens to the left.

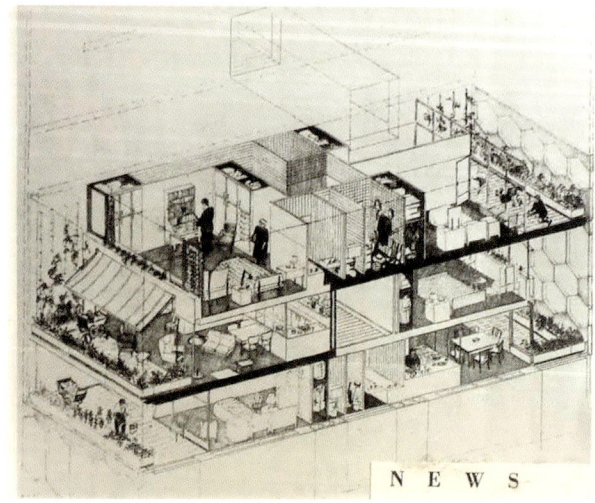

High Paddington, seen from the south-east, would have appeared as an enormous floating structure beyond the station. It would have dwarfed the existing terraces around the area.

The shadow of the Second World War was also evident in the planning of the scheme, with a note that the inhabitants would have easy access to the Underground system at Paddington, providing 'an excellent deep shelter'.[30] In fact, the deeper Underground station, on the Bakerloo line, was some distance away from the development, at the southern end of Paddington station, and would be unlikely to accommodate 8,000 people. The cost of the two World Wars was also considered, with a feeling that Britain could no longer afford to build extravagantly laid-out towns. In its straitened financial circumstances, making the best use of resources by building compact schemes like High Paddington was perhaps seen as a more economic way forward.

The Post-WWII road schemes

Even when the circumstances have seemed right for changing the layout away from London's awkward maze of irregularly laid-out streets, very little change has resulted. Going back to the aftermath of the Great Fire, when much of the City was razed, plans made by figures as notable as Sir Christopher Wren failed to go anywhere.

The next occasion that there was a substantial area of land that was clear, together with many buildings in poor condition elsewhere, was following the Second World War. The Corporation of the City of London made plans for a new ring road around the City, included in their 1944 report *Reconstruction in the City of London*. The western edge would make use of the existing wide route of Farringdon Road, Farringdon Street, and New Bridge Street, with a junction complex at Blackfriars. From here, its southern boundary

would follow the bank of the Thames between Blackfriars Bridge and London Bridge, where a large roundabout would connect to Lower Thames Street. Traffic would continue eastwards along the latter to Tower Hill, where the seventh century church of All Hallows by the Tower would be marooned on the island of a large roundabout.

The eastern side would be formed by Minories and a widened Bevis Marks, leading up to a roundabout at the junction with Bishopsgate. Heading west, the route would follow London Wall to the next major intersection, this time a diamond-shaped roundabout at Moorgate. From here, the line would cut north of London Wall, taking the line of Fore Street and crossing the bomb-damaged areas to a roundabout outside Barbican station. An alternative route used London Wall, but with the carriageways separating either side of the church of St Giles Cripplegate.

The platforms at Barbican would be covered over, with the road continuing above, forming a long lazy curve to a large junction at Holborn Circus via a T-junction with St John Street. Farringdon Road would be crossed by a new viaduct, and there would be no direct connection with the western side of the ring road.

A new report was commissioned from the architect Charles Holden and the town planning expert William Holford, based on the 1944 plans; this was published in 1947.[31] This looked at the planning opportunities for the City, together with the problems such as traffic congestion. It modified the earlier proposals in a number of ways.

The most significant of its ideas were for three routes running east-west across the City. The southern one was an upgrade of Thames Street, eventually to form a double-deck structure with local traffic serving sites such as Billingsgate Market on the lower level, and through traffic above. This would be mirrored by the northern road, which would be a completely new route. Starting in the west at a large roundabout at the end of Gray's Inn Road, it would curve north, crossing the Fleet valley to the north of Farringdon station and continue to roundabouts at Aldersgate Street, Whitecross Street, and Moorgate, following the line of London Wall. This would also be a double-deck structure, with the upper level (about 20 feet high) linking the Gray's Inn and Aldersgate Street roundabouts with no intermediate junctions.

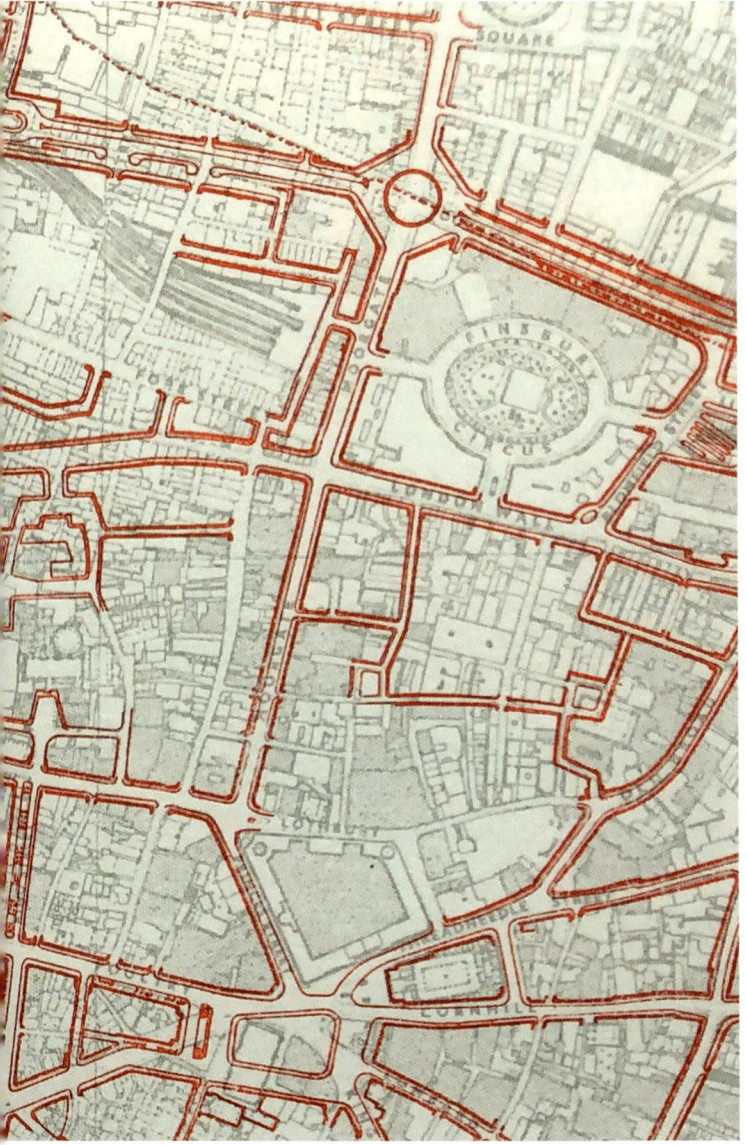

The proposed street plan for the City of London (with changes shown in red) as published in the 1947 plan by Holden and Holford for the City's reconstruction. Large roundabouts would be created at Ludgate Circus, Holborn Circus, to the east of St Paul's Cathedral, and along the route of the northern route from near Holborn across to Liverpool Street station.

The 1944 reconstruction plan focused on providing high-quality routes to the north of the City, and along the edge of the Thames, to avoid traffic clogging the narrow streets. A series of large roundabouts would have featured around the edge of the City.

At its eastern end, the viaduct would descend above the platforms of Barbican Underground station, which would be reconstructed as part of the work. The ground level road beneath the viaduct would retain junctions with side streets, and parking for over 800 cars would be accommodated beneath the upper deck on two levels. A longer-term proposal was to extend the road east from Moorgate. At ground level this would be a widening of Eldon Street, but above this a new upper level would rise to pass over Broad Street and Liverpool Street stations. A new deck would be constructed above the tracks here, to form a large station car park served by the road, with lifts to conveniently connect the station and car park.

The central route through the City would be a widening of the existing roads from Holborn Viaduct to Aldgate High Street. The former would be enlarged, with a 300-space car park excavated below, and accessed from Shoe Lane. A large new roundabout would be built at the junction of Newgate Street, Cheapside, and St Martin's-le-Grand. Probably the most radical idea, which was noted as being unlikely to happen, was to build a similar, large gyratory at the Bank junction, still a notorious bottleneck until traffic restrictions were introduced in 2017. The plan required physically moving (or demolishing) the Mansion House building (home of the City Mayor) in order to make space, and it was this that made the Bank rebuilding extremely unlikely.

The only part of the plan that ever came close to fruition was the southern boundary, which today forms Upper and Lower Thames Streets, running east from the Blackfriars Underpass as far as Byward Street and Tower Hill. The roundabouts here and at London Bridge were never built, and the dual carriageway section ends outside All Hallows church.

At around the same time, the London Country Council had commissioned the architect John Forshaw and professor of town planning, Patrick Abercrombie, to prepare plans for London after the war. As the LCC covered a far greater area than the City of London, so their plans were even more ambitious. One of the key objectives was to keep local traffic separate from the through traffic, with the latter being directed onto faster roads so as to get across London as quickly as possible. Studies were made of new highways in the USA, and of road tunnels and multi-level junctions provided in Paris.

The County of London Plan was published in 1943. The new road network that it proposed was split into two main categories. The arterial roads would have a limited number of grade-separated junctions, and would comprise two roads crossing London from north to south ('X' route), and east to west ('Y' route), a ring road (the 'B' ring), and ten radial routes (four starting on the ring road, two being continuations of the east-west route, and the remaining four being branches from the north-south cross route. The second category, termed sub-arterial roads, provided two further ring roads (one inside and one outside the arterial ring – 'A' and 'C' respectively), and another ten radial routes.

The north-south route would, in the north, start on the B ring at the north-east corner of Regent's Park and then follow the railway line to Euston. It would enter a tunnel to pass beneath the Bloomsbury area before emerging again at a large new square junction on the site of Covent Garden. The road would then continue south to another new junction that would obliterate the western end of the crescent at Aldwych, before crossing Waterloo Bridge to Elephant & Castle. Here it would split to form two of the radial routes, leading to the B ring at New Cross and Clapham.

The east-west route would run from Chelsea, along the north bank of the Thames before taking the route of Royal Hospital and Ebury Roads to Victoria. A tunnel would take it under St James's Park as far as a new junction at Charing Cross. The station here would be removed, and the Y route would continue along the Victoria Embankment as far as the Tower of London (using the same route as the City of London's planned ring road, described above). It would then continue eastwards along the northern edge of the docks to meet the B ring.

The ring roads were, if anything, even more ambitious and the amount of property that would have been lost to them would have been very significant. The innermost A ring required a tunnel beneath Hyde Park on its east side, and a new tunnel beneath the Thames just downstream of Tower Bridge. Between Paddington and Euston it would have run parallel to the Marylebone Road, cutting a swathe through residential areas. The B ring would have separated Regent's Park from Primrose Hill, and cut through residential areas such as Camden and Brixton, as well as needing a long tunnel from the Isle of Dogs to Deptford. The northern half of the C ring would have been less disruptive, as it was already in existence as the North Circular Road, although an upgrade would be needed. The southern half would require major works to widen the South Circular route, and a further tunnel would have been built under the Thames in the Beckton area.

Traffic on the arterial and sub-arterial roads was to have priority at junctions, and the number of side roads would be minimized. No buildings would be allowed to front onto the arterial roads, and service roads would be provided for shops, which would be groups together to form small shopping parades. Where the cross routes (X and Y) passed through tunnels, underground car parks would have been built with direct access, particularly near Covent Garden. This area was felt to be in need of regeneration.

As with so many of the ambitious plans for rebuilding London after the war, the cost of the schemes made them unaffordable given the state of Britain's finances. The X and Y routes were seen as unrealistic given the amount of property that would need to be purchased, and were soon dropped. At about the same time, in 1948, the LCC swapped the planned status of the A and B rings, the thinking being that if the A ring was an arterial road this would remove the need for large-scale road upgrades within its circuit. The A ring would now have only nine junctions along its length, and would be subject to a minimum speed limit.

This new proposal lasted just two years. The LCC was pushing the Government to safeguard the route as part of its planning, with the intention being to start construction once London's housing stock had been repairs and replaced. However, in May 1950 the Minister of Town and Country Planning stated that the plans were unaffordable and killed them.

Monorails to Heathrow

In 1958, with the plans for the M4 motorway between London and Heathrow Airport still on the drawing board, no fewer than three groups were pushing the Government to approve their schemes for monorails lining the capital with its airport. The Government asked all three to submit more detailed plans, including costings, so that they could be compared and evaluated.[32]

One scheme was proposed by International Monorail Ltd. This was similar in construction to the Regent Street monorail (see p76), in that the cars would be suspended from two bogies, each fitted with pneumatic tyres running inside a large box-girder beam. Lateral guide wheels would also be provided, and to reduce the risk of fire, the tyres would be filled with non-flammable nitrogen. The connections between the bogies and the car would pass through a slot in the bottom of the beam. Noise would be reduced by the motors and bogies being enclosed, and the electrical connection would also be contained in the beam, with sliding pick-ups on the top of each bogie.

For the proposed system to Heathrow, there would be no intermediate stops, and a loop at each end to turn the cars. The suggested route followed the Great West Road from the West London Air Terminal (near Earl's Court). Coloured light signals would be used, possibly repeated in the drivers' cabs. The only points would be at the depot, which was probably as well since they would involve pivoting entire sections of the beam, and driving through very slowly.

Probably influenced by the concept of air travel, the cars were to resemble planes without wings and tails, and would be finished in unpainted stainless steel, which was the latest fad. Seating 60, as well as their luggage, the cars would travel at up to 75 mph, gently swinging outwards on curves (but with damping to prevent them from swinging too wildly). A driver would be in a cab at the front, controlling either a single car or multiple cars operating as a train. The luggage compartment would be at the other end, and bags and suitcases would be loaded onto trolleys that would roll into this compartment. Smaller items could be placed onto racks above the seats. Boarding and alighting would be via four doors, placed on both sides at each end of the cars.

A model of the system was placed on show at the Science Museum in May 1956.

The second scheme was from Air-Rail Ltd. The cars would straddle a large concrete rail, with the passenger compartment above this level and the luggage below, in separate compartments either side of the rail. The intention was to construct the line above the existing railway out of Victoria station, following the route via Clapham Junction, Putney, Richmond, and Feltham before heading into the airport and running round the west side to reach the centre.

One of the ingenious points about this scheme was that as well as the equipment to move the cars along the concrete rail, they would also have smaller road wheels underneath. As they approached Heathrow they would disengage from the rail and be driven conventionally through the airport tunnel to reach the terminal building in the centre. As the monorail could not cross the runways or taxiways this avoided the need to construct another tunnel. If check-in was carried out at a terminal in Victoria then the cars could be driven right up to the planes.

The cars themselves were to be constructed of lightweight magnesium alloy and plastics, and powered by diesel engines. The promoters suggested a running speed of 100 mph on the monorail track, although this was to be built to allow future vehicles to travel at up to 250 mph. Each would hold 50 passengers with luggage, with the latter being loaded onto pallets for convenient loading and unloading.

The third system seems to have left no trace in the historic record. However, the other two persisted. International Monorail included French partners, and the German firm of Alweg backed the Air-Rail scheme. Government officials travelled

The Air-Rail scheme, illustrating (top) the monorail structure above the existing railway from Victoria, (bottom left) the vehicles driving on their own wheels, potentially right up to the plane, and (bottom right) the appearance of the monorail when passing through countryside on its way to Heathrow.

overseas to inspect different trial monorails, and a full-size prototype of the Air-Rail system was suggested for Basildon in 1959 as a trial of the technology.

The debate rumbled on into the 1960s, with no conclusion being reached. Conventional railway links were also proposed, and seen as being less risky as the technology was known and understood. By 1966, London Transport was suggesting an extension of the Piccadilly line: again, known technology, even if more expensive than either a surface railway or a monorail. The plans for monorails faded out, and were replaced by arguments between LT and BR over their respective railway schemes, with LT eventually winning with the opening of the Piccadilly line extension to the airport in 1977.

The Monster of Piccadilly Circus

Proposals for the rebuilding of Piccadilly Circus pop up throughout the twentieth century. Norman Shaw, the architect of the New Scotland Yard building on the Embankment, proposed a rearrangement that, whilst tidying up the layout, upset people by adding a new building in the centre, thus rather removing the concept of the Circus.

Most of the other suggestions from before the Second World War involved alterations to the north and eastern sides to make the Circus rectangular. It had originally been a circle when laid out by John Nash, but this was lost when Shaftesbury Avenue was added in 1886. In 1910, an unsolicited proposal was for the area to be renamed Edward VII Square, as a memorial to the late King, with a large rectangular island in the centre featuring a statue of the monarch. The statue (incorrectly known as Eros) that had occupied the centre position would be relocated to a park. Nothing was ever done about this plan.

Around the same time, two other plans featured pedestrians being moved to a level above the Circus. One plan placed a roof above the whole of the space, with a pedestrian level at first-floor level and traffic remaining below. Another proposed arched bridges over the roads leading into the Circus, allowing pedestrians to cross between the shops who would now have entrances and colonnaded walkways at the same height. Escalators would allow people to move between street and first-floor levels.

The most controversial plan for the area became known to the public in 1959. On 27 October, plans were unveiled to transform Piccadilly Circus. An office tower, 172 ft tall, was to be built on the north side of the junction, where the massive illuminated advertisements were placed. The new tower would host the advertisements on its sides, some 100 ft high, with an enormous permanent crane on the roof in order to lift them into position; the crane was to be illuminated as a building feature. A podium building at the base of the tower would run along the length of the site. This was not the whim of a property developer, but a £7 million plan which had received permission from the authorities and which was poised to go ahead. It was reckoned that 120 weeks would be needed to clear the site and complete the redevelopment.

The plan had been put together by a developer called Jack Cotton, who had bought all of the buildings on the site, and worked with the London County Council architects to design the new development. Everything was ready to go when Cotton called his press conference and showed off a model of the scheme.

The reaction from Londoners was immediate, and they were appalled. *The Spectator* nicknamed the scheme 'The Monster of Piccadilly Circus', and angry letters were published in *The Times*, whose architectural correspondent described the buildings as "insensitive and banal". MPs questioned how the scheme could be approved, and with the pressure building, the Minister for Housing reluctantly called the scheme in for review, ostensibly over the rooftop crane, which had not been part of the approved design. Many of his fellow parliamentarians protested vociferously against the plans, objecting to the poor quality of the design and the lack of integration with the rest of the site.

A public enquiry was called, which started at about the same time that Cotton submitted a revised proposal in response to the criticism. The changes were minor, omitting the crane and altering the advertisements. No one thought that the fundamental problem was addressed though, and further criticisms of the plan was made. An American architect described the scheme as "designed by ghosts, with ghosts, for ghosts".[33] What was needed, many thought, was a masterplan for the whole Piccadilly Circus area.

The Minister announced his decision on 20 May 1960: rejection. The development "would fall below the high standard [that the] public expect". There were also problems over the amount of car parking provided, and the effect on the skyline around the

Jack Cotton's building would have loomed over Piccadilly Circus without enhancing the quality of the architecture. The style of the building would have dated quickly.

Circus. In a comment that must have galled Cotton, he also noted that had the press conference not been held in October 1959, the development would probably have gone ahead uncontested.

The London County Council appointed the architect Sir William Holford to prepare a comprehensive plan for the whole of the Circus. His first scheme proposed a raised piazza with a tower on the south side of the Circus, but this was then replaced with a complete reimagining of the area with a large rectangular space at its heart. Tall buildings surrounded the site, and traffic would flow on the north side, with 'Eros' on a raised piazza occupying the southern side of the space. The intention was that the piazza could be flooded and frozen in winter, to form a small ice skating rink.

Away from this piazza, pedestrians would use raised walkways to get around, with stairs and escalators connecting between levels. A bridge provided a walkway between the north and south sides of the space, crossing above the piazza. A slender tower 180-ft tall would rise from the Criterion site, topped with a sculpture of a pleated ruff, once known as a 'piccadill', from which the area took its name.

Despite the backing of the LCC, in September 1963 this plan also floundered, this time on the grounds that insufficient space was provided for traffic. Holford was furious, and threatened to resign. He stated that it was not possible for the Circus to remain an attraction whilst also enabling it to take increasing volumes of traffic.

Holford's threat was not carried out, and he continued to work on plans for the area. It was not until 1968 that a new proposal was made public. He had reconciled the two requirements by creating a two-level Circus. Traffic would occupy the street level, and 26 feet above this would be the replacement pedestrian piazza. The pedestrian deck would continue into Regent Street, around the Quadrant and up towards Oxford Circus.

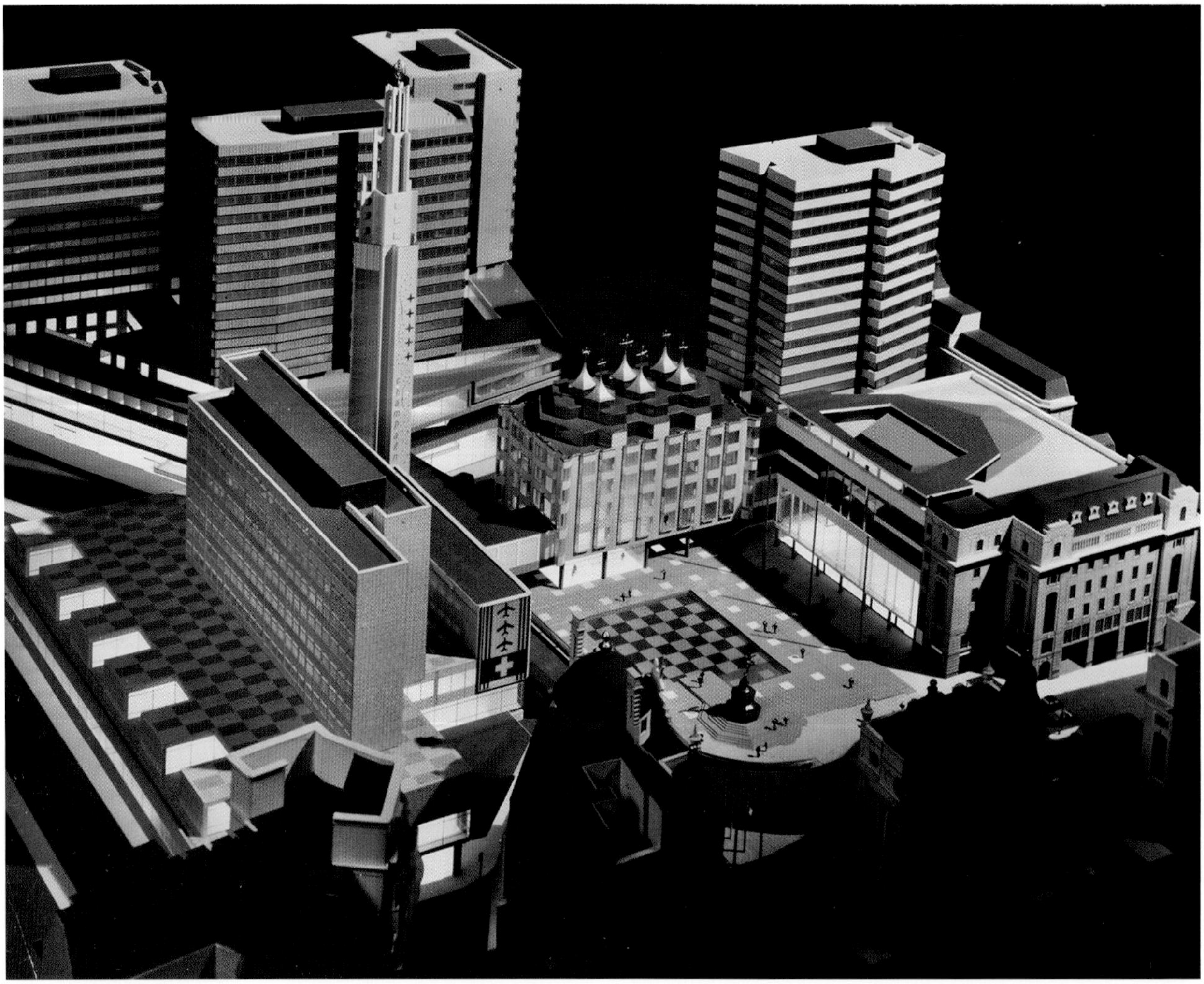

Opposite page top: One of the schemes proposed by William Holford in 1961 extended the cinema out from the Monico site across part of the circus, with traffic passing beneath.

Opposite page bottom: Holford's scheme from around 1963, showing the tower topped by a stylized piccadill on the north side of the Circus. Regent Street is at the bottom of this model.

Above: This model of one of William Holford's schemes for Piccadilly Circus from around 1969 clearly shows the existing ground-level area half-covered by a new pedestrian plaza with the existing statue at its centre, and range of new buildings around three sides. To the east, the block between Shaftesbury Avenue and Leicester Square would be redeveloped with a pedestrian deck as far as Charing Cross Road.

Roads below

The success of the underground railways in London showed that traffic could be safely accommodated beneath the surface. And if trains could do it, why not trams and cars too? In 1906 the Kingsway Tram Subway opened, linking the trams networks north and south of the river Thames. The plans for St Paul's Bridge a few years later (see p14) included a similar tram subway to the east of St Paul's Cathedral to reduce traffic conflict at Cheapside. Skip forward to the 1960s, and a few road tunnels were planned for sections of the Ringways (see p70) where it was necessary to avoid demolition of surface property.

A more extensive tunnel proposal for 1972 was called the Underways,[34] and was based on a paper presented to the International Road Federation in 1966.[35] The plan was for motor traffic to pass beneath London. Motorists just wishing to get from one side to another could use a tunnel, rather than congesting the surface, and those whose destination was in London did not always need to have their car at the destination. Underground car parks, linked to the road tunnels, would have lifts and escalators to take their occupants to the surface.

Six tunnels were proposed (three running north-south, and three east-west), each to be 60 feet in diameter and placed at a depth of 80 – 160 ft. Each tunnel would contain two three-lane roads (plus hard shoulders), one above the other. Space was also provided for travelators to transport people between the car parks and surface access points, and, as was typical for many transport schemes of the day, there would be a monorail in each direction in some tunnels. Ventilation ducts would occupy the awkward spaces left in the tunnels, as well as utility ducts.

The twelve portals were allocated numbers starting from T1 on the west side of London and running clockwise. The six tunnels had the following routes:

Between		and	
T1 (west)	M4 (Chiswick Roundabout)	T7 (east)	A13 (Barking)
T2 (west)	A40 (Hanger Lane gyratory)	T6 (east)	M11 (South Woodford)
T3 (north)	M1 (Staples Corner)	T11 (south)	M23 (Mitcham)
T4 (north)	A406 (Finchley)	T10 (south)	Parkway East (Brixton)
T5 (north)	A10 (Cambridge roundabout)	T9 (south)	Bromley
T12 (west)	A3 (Wandsworth)	T8 (east)	A2/A20 (Eltham)

At the crossing point of each pair of tunnels an underground intersection would be built, allowing vehicles to switch between routes. The space between adjacent parallel tunnels in the central area would be occupied by the car parks, which would consist of a series of parallel tunnels. These would also be of 60-ft diameter, presumably for ease of, providing six levels of parking, and enough would be built to provide for approximately 100,000 cars.

Traffic would enter the Underways through around 27 portals encircling London (the diagrams in the booklet that was published are not entirely consistent on this point). Each would provide access to a tunnel, containing two 2-lane roads, one above the other. These tunnels would converge on the main tunnels as they approached the centre of London at a series of underground junctions. The portals would be located on the major roads approaching London: for example, portal E4 would be on the A40 at East Acton, portal E7 would allow traffic to and from the M1 at Staples Corner, and portal E11 would be for access to and from the A10 at Tottenham. Some of the portals were on the planned Ringways, and hence if viewed on a modern map appear to be marooned in back streets. That at Willesden Junction (E5) would have

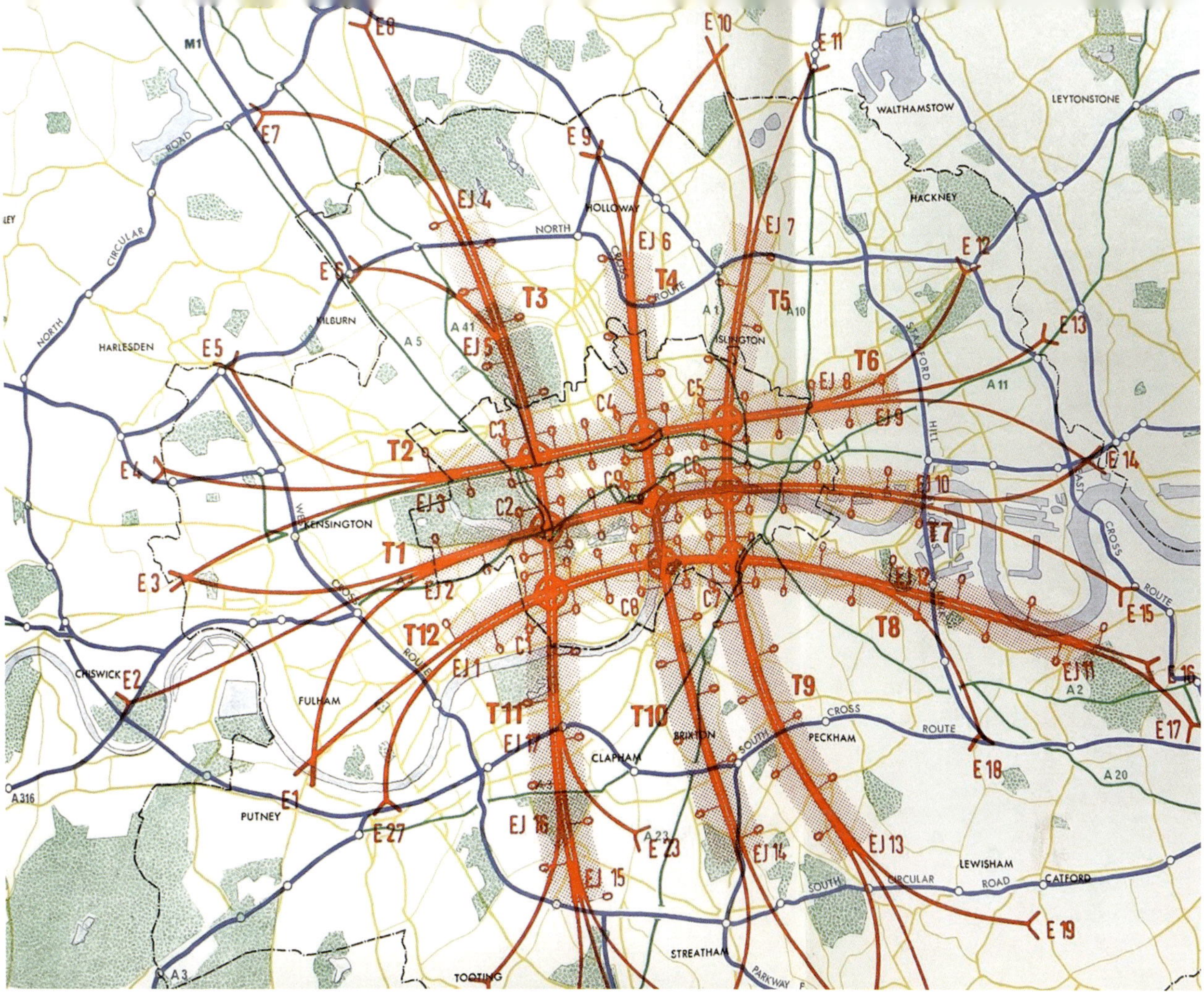

A plan of the Underways scheme, showing the six main tunnels forming a grid beneath central London, and splitting into their distributor tunnels at each end. Some of the planned Ringways are also shown.

A cross-section of one of the main Underway tunnels, showing how the two carriageways, monorails, pedestrian travelators, and ventilation would be fitted in.

57

linked to the North Cross Route, E12 – E17 were on the East Cross Route, and E24 on the southern section of Ringway 2 at Norbury.

The booklet went into a lot of detail about the benefits, pointing out the saving of land over similar construction of surface roads, the reduction in accidents with traffic confined to single direction tunnels, and the improvement to London's air. They glossed over the complexity of building such large tunnels – five times the diameter of the London Underground running tunnels – and the potential for ground settlement above. The estimated cost of the Underways was calculated at £2.4 billion, although against this was set benefits of £1.5 billion through not needing to build Ringway 1, reduced congestion, and other factors, bringing it down to £890 million. This cost was compared to a hypothetical cost of providing the same length of road and number of parking spaces at surface level, given as £6·75 billion, even though this was clearly never going to happen.

The Underways would not be free to use. A charge of 20p was proposed for using them in any 24-hour period (whether driving through or parking), covering one hour's parking. Further parking would be 10p per hour between 07.30 and 19.30, and 2·5p otherwise. The author of the report estimated that this would raise £128 million each year which would repay the overall £890 million cost in 10 years, or the full £2·4 billion in 23 years.

The plans had support in Parliament, with Lord Popplewell speaking in favour in the House of Lords, and the MP Sir Ronald Russell in the Commons; both also submitted questions to the Minister of Transprt about the scheme.

The Ministry of Transport investigated the plans with their author, as well as consulting other engineers. They concluded that the costs were likely to be double the estimate, and noted that 'to involve so heavy a concentration of national resource into a limited area seems financially impracticable'.[36] The technical challenge of building such large tunnels on this scale was described as 'formidable' and 'of doubtful feasibility'. The largest bored tunnel in 2021 is the Tuen Mun – Chek Lap Kok Link in Hong Hong, with is 17·6 m (57 ft 8 ins) diameter, so fifty years later no tunnel 60 ft wide has been bored, especially through soft ground such as that beneath London.

Given the clear rejection of the Underways scheme, it therefore appears strange to find that in October 1972, the Greater London Council (GLC) commissioned the engineering consultancies of Mott, Hay and Anderson and Sir William Halcrow and Partners, both experts in tunnelling, to prepare a report into the feasibility of building road tunnels under London. They noted that the combination of rising land prices, improvements in tunnelling technology, and concerns about the environment had caused the GLC to think that this could be a solution to the problems that had caused the cancellation of much of the Ringway schemes. It focused on south London though, and the use of smaller tunnels than the Underways, including the use of elliptical cross-sections to reduce the amount of excavation.

The report,[37] published just over a year later, was remarkably detailed. It examined the varied geology beneath London and the cost of different tunnelling processes that might be required by this. Ventilation and lighting systems were considered, as well as the configuration of curves, gradients, and signs to establish what good practice would look like. Most interestingly it looked at how junctions could be made safely in tunnels, giving a number of different designs, including an intriguing anti-clockwise roundabout that took advantage of the ability to 'roll' one tunnel over another so that traffic would always enter and leave roads from the left. It also provided two detailed studies for tunnels in south London.

Scheme 1 was for a new road linking Loughborough Junction to St John's, via Peckham. This followed the course of part of the abandoned South Cross Route (part of Ringway 1), and where the existing alternative was (and remains) a series of single carriageway roads with many junctions that suffer from significant congestion.

The road would be a three-lane dual carriageway with a single intermediate interchange at surface level just south of Peckham Rye station. Either side of this, it would run in twin tunnels.

The western tunnel would pass beneath Denmark Hill, surfacing just west of Ruskin Park; the eastern tunnel would resurface to join the A2210 Brookmill Road between St John's and Lewisham. It was felt necessary to provide a junction in Peckham, and the difficult ground conditions meant that this would be easiest to build at surface level. The 3 km-long eastern tunnel would have an intermediate ventilation shaft next to Brockley station, and all the tunnel portals on both tunnels would also have ventilation plant. The consultants estimated that this scheme would take around 5½ years to build, at a total cost of £132·6 million. Some 300 houses would be required, and 554 would need noise insulation to be installed. By comparison, the report noted that building the road at the surface would cost just over half (£70·1 million), but would cause 564 house demolitions and 1,520 to have noise insulation fitted.

The second scheme in the report was for a tunnel linking Battersea with Brixton. Two possible routes were considered: a direct route (2A) and one with a longer tunnel but providing an interchange towards Nine Elms (2B), which was preferred. The western portals for the two three-lane tunnels would take traffic from a junction on Battersea Park Road, and head east to a sunken roundabout on the site of Stewart's Lane Railway Depot, from which a spur road would connect north to another junction on Battersea Park Road, this time opposite the power station. Through traffic on the main route would pass beneath the roundabout in the tunnels to the next junction, where slip roads in tunnel would link with Clapham High Street. The tunnels would continue east, rising to the surface just west of Brixton station and climbing onto a viaduct to pass over the station and other railway lines. Although the intention at this end was not declared, it appears that the viaduct would then connect with Coldharbour Lane.

There would also be a connection with Balham High Street, but not involving any tunnels. A pair of slip roads would run between the Brixton portals and Balham High Street, allowing traffic a faster route between the two points as a side-effect of the tunnel.

Unlike Scheme 1, the tunnel was planned to be elliptical in cross-section, reducing the amount of tunnelling required whilst allowing up to four lanes, which was necessary at the various underground junctions to allow drivers space to switch lane safely. The slip road tunnels would all have two lanes.

The duration of the works to build Scheme 2 was estimated to be the same as for Scheme 1, but the cost would be rather less at £94 million. Around 700 properties would need to be cleared, but only 21 would need noise insulation. The equivalent surface route was estimated to have a cost of £81.6 million, 1,145 properties cleared, and 816 houses insulated, as well as affecting several conservation areas.

Both schemes (shown below) were hypothetical, and were chosen in part because the costs and effects of providing the same links on the surface were already known. It seems likely that the GLC was seriously considering the possibility of building one or both though, as they were still keen to provide a good east-west connecting route in inner London, south of the Thames. With both schemes built, a short length of connecting route between Brixton and Loughborough Junction would have sufficed to form a good bypass for south London as a replacement for the South Cross Route.

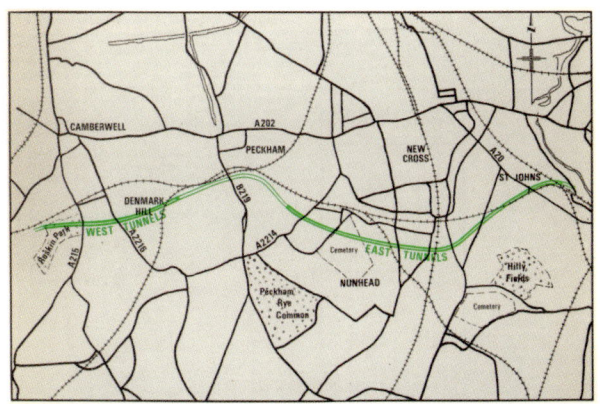

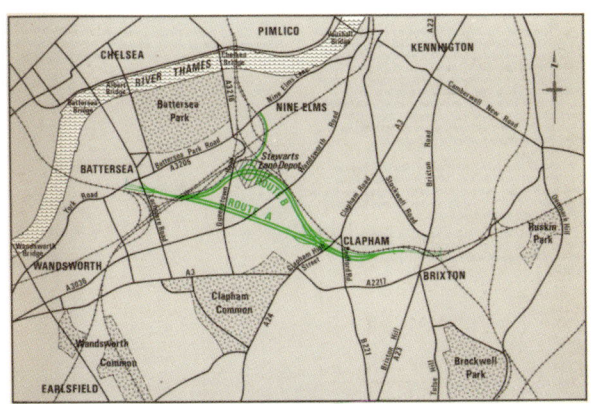

The City of London Pedways

In the 1960s, as the City of London started the process of redeveloping the large sites that had been cleared by bombing in WWII, the private car was seen as the future of transport. New roads were planned across the sites, which would also involve demolishing undamaged buildings to form new routes across the City (see p48). The planners felt that it would be a good idea to keep pedestrians and traffic apart. The French architect Le Corbusier had proposed such an idea in the 1920s, with pedestrians occupying a podium deck above the road traffic.[38] The concept had been used on London's South Bank for the 1951 Festival of Britain, and was thought to be a success, with elevated walkways linking different pavilions within the site.[39]

The construction of the Barbican in the decade from 1965 incorporated a series of highwalks – pedestrian routes at first floor level that crossed over roads on bridges. At convenient traffic centres, such as road junctions and stations, stairs led down to ground level. The southern boundary of the site was London Wall, a new dual carriageway that was intended to stretch westwards to Holborn Circus, and which was spanned by three bridges (four were originally intended), since the road was not intended for use by those on foot. Four office towers flanked the road, sitting on a raised podium which formed part of the walkways, and the building entrances were placed at the podium level too.

Architects of other buildings in the City were encouraged, through the planning process, to incorporate space for pedways in their structures, with the intention of linking them up by bridges once there were sufficient in number. Until then, the spaces could be temporarily glazed and used as office space. The problem, however, was that there was no single plan for the pedway system, with it instead forming organically as buildings were redeveloped. In total, the City planners envisaged a network of 48 km of pedways, spanning the City from Chancery Lane in the west to Minories in the east, and from Aldersgate Street in the north right the way down to the Thames.

The piecemeal approach taken to the construction of the pedway system was part of the reason for its failure. The network was not developed in a comprehensive way that led to it becoming increasingly useful to pedestrians.

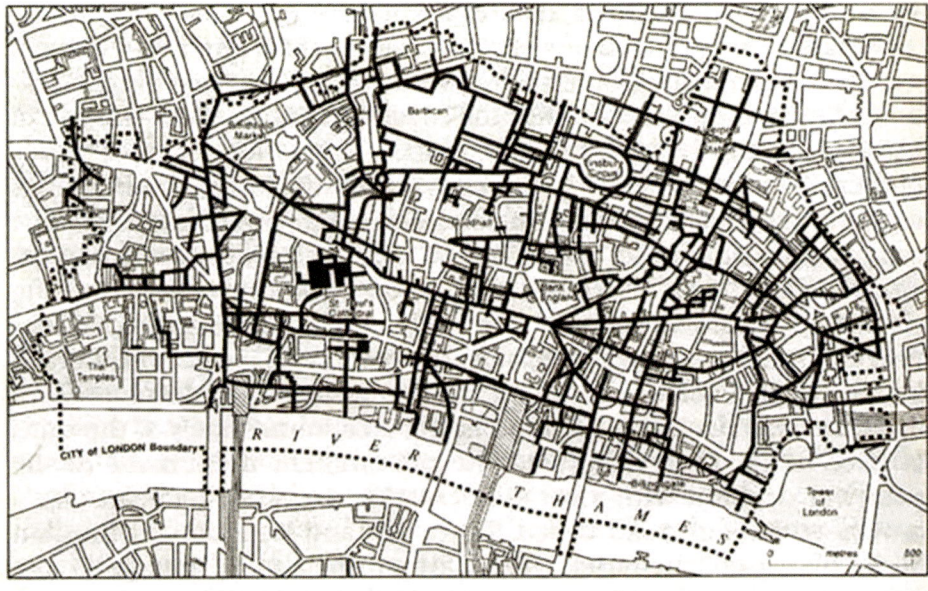

The intended pedway network in 1963 would have provided a dense network of routes above traffic level throughout the City of London.

Instead different sections meant that users had to go up and down flights of stairs, which acts as a deterrent. The developers of the buildings that were compelled to include sections of pedway had no incentive to spend any more than the bare minimum on the facilities, leading to them often being bleak, windswept corridors. Sections were built that had no other connections, such as a bridge over Bishopsgate at the NatWest Tower that was never used, and subsequently demolished. The brutalist architecture, typified by the Barbican, also led to the system feeling unsafe for its users. Over time, sections were closed down when development caused a section to become a path to nowhere. Too late, facilities such as shops, banks, and restaurants were provided at pedway level, with incentives having to be provided to the occupiers to move up to the first floor. In general, these did not last for long.

Another problem was the legal status of the pedways. They were built and paid for by private developers, but existed as public space. Responsibility for lighting and cleaning them was unclear, and if one thing is guaranteed to deter pedestrians it is a poorly lit, unclean environment which will inevitably be perceived as threatening.

Pedways do still exist today though, primarily around the Barbican, but in a few isolated outposts nearer to the Thames as well. Some of the original sections have been removed with the redevelopment of buildings and the demolition of unused footbridges. New areas have been added through. The construction of Alban Gate, a large development that sits astride London Wall and which opened in 1992, added new routes to the network, together with escalators linking down to Wood Street and restaurants at the pedway level, providing an incentive to use them. In 2018, London Wall Place was constructed to the east of Alban Gate, and added a number of new pedways linking to both the Barbican, and the south side of London Wall. These were deliberately designed to be high-quality public spaces incorporating seating and gardens, and making use of different materials. The bridges, in pre-oxidized Corten steel, contrast with the raw concrete of the original structures.

The next addition to the pedways network will be at 21 Moorfields, another new building above the Crossrail station at Moorgate. More escalators will carry pedestrians up to a new highwalk, replacing a pair that used to exist in a claustrophobic passageway alongside the earlier station building.

Although the pedways are only a shadow of the original plan, and thus deserving of a place here, they are certainly not a failed concept. It will be interesting to see if their reinvigoration continues.

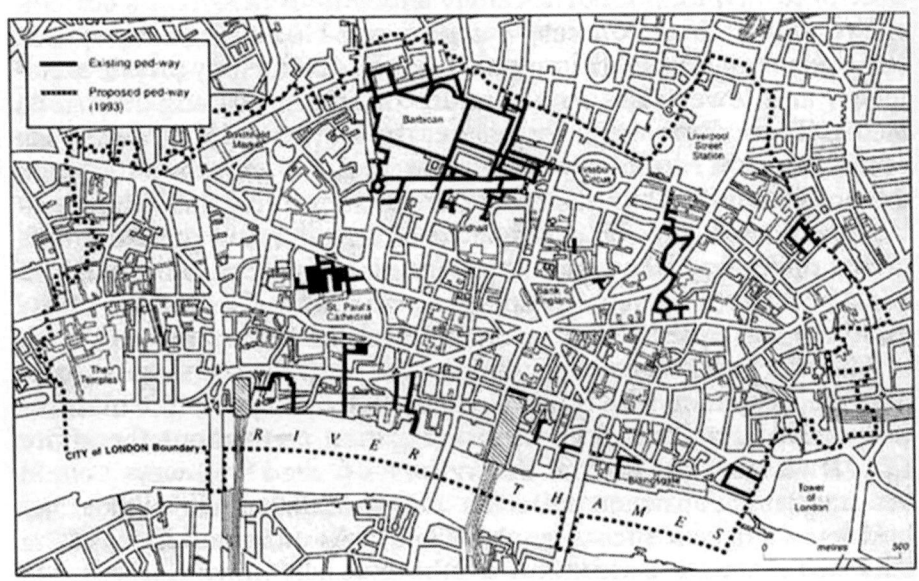

By 1992, only a fraction of the intended network had been realized, much of this in and around the Barbican. It looked as though the remaining routes were unlikely to survive for much longer.

Plans for Westminster

The seat of British government is located in Westminster, and particularly the area south of Trafalgar Square, along the road called Whitehall, and continuing along the Thames south of Parliament Square and also westwards along the southern edge of St James's Park. The Palace of Whitehall, created by Henry VIII from around 1531, was destroyed by fire in 1698, leaving only the Banqueting House standing on the eastern side. In 1834, the original Palace of Westminster, the seat of Parliament, also burned down and was subsequently replaced by the current Gothic building, designed by Sir Charles Barry and Augustus Pugin. In style, it matches Westminster Abbey, which is just across the road.

One of the major government buildings along Whitehall is the Foreign Office, with its entrance on King Charles Street. After its completion it originally housed four government departments; the Foreign, India, Colonial, and Home Offices. A competition was run by the Government in 1856-7 for a new Foreign Office building on the site, and a design by Sir George Gilbert Scott was chosen, despite only coming third. However, the building that we see today was not his original proposal.

In keeping with the style of the times, Scott produced a Gothic design, and this was favoured by the head of the Board of Works, which explains why Scott was awarded the commission. Shortly afterwards it was decided to erect a new building for the India Office adjacent to the Foreign Office, and to avoid a potential clash of styles this was also awarded to Scott, who gave some of the work to his fellow architect Matthew Digby Wyatt.

Work on the design was progressing through 1859, despite opposition from some MPs, including Lord Palmerston. A general election saw Palmerston become Prime Minister on 1 July, and from this moment the Gothic design was doomed. Palmerston told Scott that his design was "a regular mongrel affair", and to redesign it in the Italianate style.[40]

Scott was not happy with this, as he had to start again – almost from scratch. He regretted not advancing his Gothic design fast enough so that when Palmerston had become Prime Minister the design would have been a *fait accompli*. After discussing the matter with Wyatt and other friends, Scott decided to go ahead with the redesign, and spent much of the next year creating it. This period included a trip to Paris to view other Italianate buildings.

In June 1861 both the Gothic and Italianate designs were put on display in the tea-room of the House of Commons for MPs to examine. Following a debate on 8 July, a vote was held and the Italianate design was successful by a majority of 93 votes.[41] This was the design that was used for the building, which was completed in 1868. In the same year, Scott was appointed as architect for the Home and Colonial Office buildings, which were on the site between Whitehall and the Foreign and India Offices. Once completed in 1875, the four buildings formed a single block in the heart of the Government area of London.

One problem that exercised the Victorians was how to honour the nation's great people. Traditionally they were interred in Westminster Abbey, but this was getting full. Various ideas for a suitable National Monument were proposed, for different locations in London, and a Royal Commission was even created in 1891 to consider the problem – although they failed to reach a conclusion. The most extravagant was the 1904 scheme for the site between the Abbey and Parliament, created by John Seddon and Edward Lamb. Both had previously designed separate schemes for such a building, and in the early 1900s joined forces to create a new plan.

The Imperial Monumental Halls and Tower was to comprise a long hall with a double transept at its southern end, and a single transept at the north which would be linked to a memorial tower. This in turn would have a cloistered arcade connecting it with the Abbey, next to the Chapter House. The main hall would be on the site that is today

The tower of the Imperial Monumental Halls would have rather overshadowed the Palace of Westminster, and in this illustration of the time, seems to be out of scale with the rest of the buildings in the area.

occupied by College Green, best known for hosting the media when reporting from Parliament. The mediæval Jewel Tower would have been kept, although it would have been awkwardly squeezed in between the main hall and the tower, and this is the reason for only one north transept.

The building would be in the same Gothic style as the Palace of Westminster, which would have been rather overshadowed. The main Monumental Hall would have been a similar height to the Abbey, and would have had three spired towers. The Memorial Tower, however, would have been 550 feet high; over 200 feet higher than either of the Palace towers, although the effect would have been slightly lessened by the openwork at the top. To prevent the Abbey from looking too small, a new tower was suggested for it, rising from its central crossing. The intention was that funerals of British worthies would take place at Westminster Abbey, before they would be carried in procession through to the Monumental Hall for interment.

The plans were exhibited for a brief period at a studio near Sloane Square, and were described with understatement as being 'a grandiose suggestion for an English Walhalla' by *The Builder*,[42] although the author went on to state that 'the immense scale proposed for the tower has a little too much of "megalomania" about it'. The architects accepted that it would be an expensive undertaking and considered that it could be built in a number of phases. They noted that 'grandeur of scale and costly execution would, of course, be essential to the structure'.[43] It is quite understandable that despite the beauty of the drawings that they produced, nothing ever came of the Imperial Monumental Halls and Tower.

Sixty years later, another grandiose scheme for Westminster was begun. This time, it would involve substantial demolition as well, clearing the sites of the Treasury and Foreign Office buildings on the west side of Whitehall, and the corresponding block on the east side of the street as far as the Victoria Embankment. In their place would rise a gargantuan Government office complex, mainly consisting of buildings running from north to south, with a huge east-west connecting block crossing them all and spanning Whitehall. A series of courtyards would be formed between the buildings, which would have a stepped profile on their north side to maximize the light entering the offices. The buildings would house several departments in open-plan offices, giving them room to expand and contract as necessary.

The architect for the scheme was Sir Leslie Martin, a modernist who had previously designed the Royal Festival Hall and the Bloomsbury Centre (which also uses the stepped profile). Like both of these, the new Government complex would be brutalist in style, deploying mass concrete. Sir Leslie was appointed by the Government to prepare a scheme in 1964, in part to respond to a number of proposals to redevelop individual sites in the area.[44]

The buildings would not be high, so as not to overshadow the Palace of Westminster and Westminster Abbey. To provide sufficient office space, a large amount of the area would need to be covered with buildings, and so the courtyards were essential to provide daylight light inside. The south-eastern corner of the building would have a shopping concourse at ground level, linked with Westminster Underground station. This would provide a pedestrian route between the embankment and Parliament Street.[45]

The building was only part of the scheme, which was to provide a semi-pedestrianized 'parliamentary precinct' in the area between Trafalgar Square, the Thames, Horseferry Road, and bounded on the west by Horse Guards Road, Storey's Gate, Great Smith Street, and Marsham Street. At Parliament Square, the block on the west side that today includes the Supreme Court would be swept away to provide more open space. The traffic that passed through the area on a north-south axis would be diverted into a road tunnel along the edge of the Thames, forming a continuation of the Victoria Embankment southwards to Lambeth Bridge. Within the new embankment vehicles would use a two-lane dual carriageway, which would rise back to the existing street level alongside Whitehall Gardens. The roof of the tunnel would be planted and paved, and would provide six acres of new public space, and 2·3 acres of additional terrace space for the Parliamentary estate.

This scheme would involve significant disruption and so a phased approach was planned. Diverting the traffic was the first goal, involving the construction of the new embankment and tunnel. The first phase of building would take place on the Underground station site; next the Treasury building would be replaced, and finally the Foreign Office in around 1980.

It might seem surprising today that little fuss was raised about the demolition of the latter two buildings, but there was less consideration given to architectural heritage (and especially that of the Victorian age) in the 1960s – recall, for example, the plans to demolish St Pancras station. The full-page article in *The Times* had only a small corner giving the views of the Victorian Society, which preferred retaining the façade of the Foreign Office (but not the interior), and made no comment about the loss of the Edwardian Treasury building.

The Civic Trust requested that the plans be considered by a public inquiry, noting that a cost of £100 million had been suggested, and that any scheme costing this much deserved to be thoroughly reviewed. As it involved the redevelopment of Government property it was exempt from the need to go through formal planning controls, and hence an enquiry could take the place of this process. The Government, however,

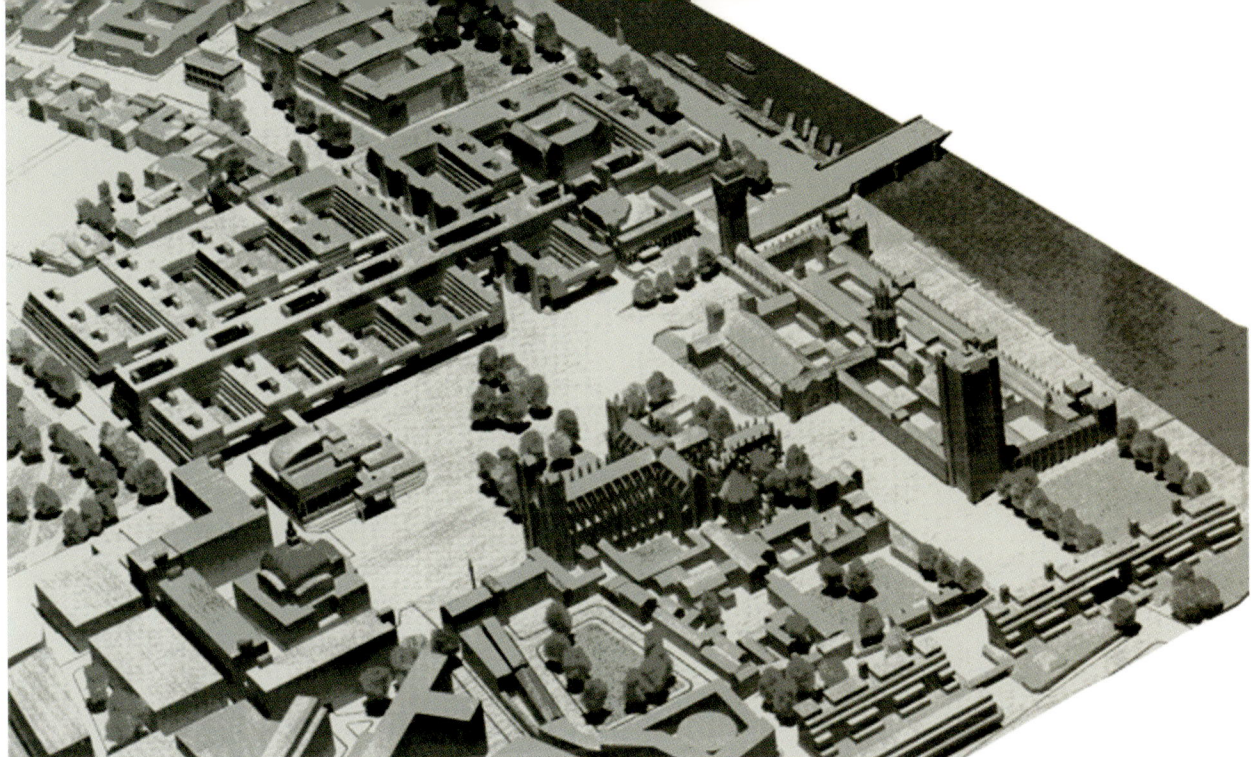

rejected this call,⁴⁶ even though members of the House of Lords were recommending it "before destroying one of the finest urban landscapes in the world".⁴⁷

Despite this, the Government was determined to continue, and was particularly keen to get rid of the Foreign Office building, designed by Sir George Gilbert Scott and completed in 1868, with Lord Mitchison, the representative of the Ministry of Land and Natural Resources telling his fellow peers that "it was definite that the Foreign Office was coming down."⁴⁸ He was wrong. Ultimately the cost of the scheme defeated it, and the Government quietly put the plan to bed.

Above: A model of Sir Leslie Martin's monolithic government complex stretching from the Thames in the east to St James's Park in the west.

Left: Another illustration of the government complex, with the shape of the proposed buildings shown in grey. The northern edge faces Downing Street and the MoD Main Building, and the block to the south (along the bottom of the picture) borders Great Peter Street and Great Smith Street.

Redevelopment of Soho

The architect Geoffrey Jellicoe, together with Edward Mills and Ove Arup proposed a complete reconstruction of the Soho area of London in 1955. The proposal was created through their work as the Glass Age Development Committee, a body created by Pilkington Glass in 1937 to promote the use of glass as a building material. The scheme involved a new pedestrian level at rooftop height, with six 24-storey towers rising above, and glass-bottomed canals following the pattern of the streets below. An open-air swimming pool would have been placed above the central market area, with the architects noting that "From below the bathers will appear like fish". The *Architectural Review* merely concluded "An age of naïve optimism".

Even with glass bottoms to the canals, the streets of Soho would have been incredibly gloomy beneath the podium of the proposed redevelopment of the area.

Covent Garden rebuilding

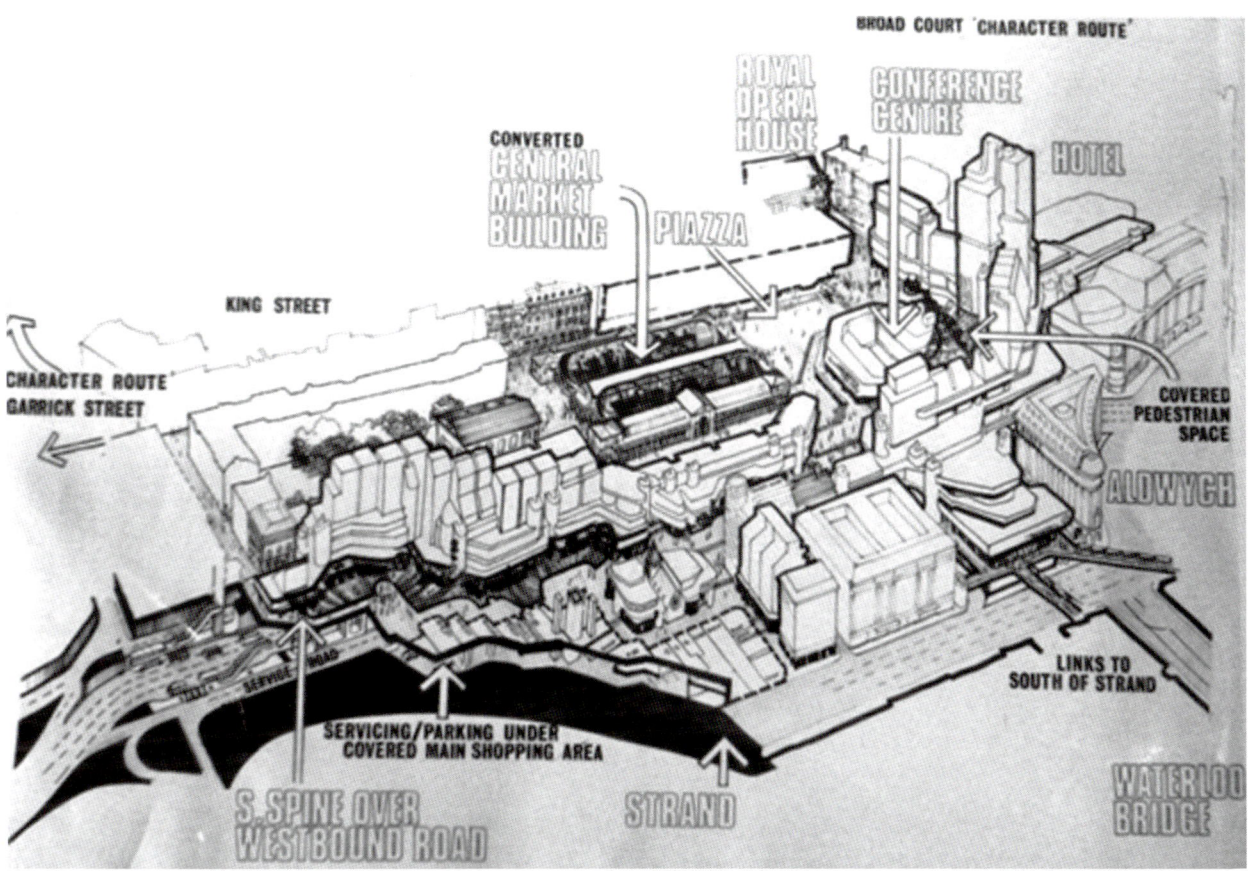

In the late 1960s, the Greater London Council planned for the historic fruit and vegetable market at Covent Garden to be moved to a site in Nine Elms. Urban planners soon saw this as an opportunity to redevelop the entire area south of Shaftesbury Avenue. An international conference centre would be built on the site of the Flower Market (now the London Transport Museum), and many of the 18th and 19th century buildings would be cleared to make way for new shows and offices above an underground service area. The Strand would take westbound traffic only, with a new underground road a little to the north taking eastbound traffic. The plans were published in 1968, and protests began soon after. These, together with a change of political control of the GLC in 1973, caused the scheme to be scrapped.

An isometric cutaway drawing of the proposed almost total reconstruction of the Covent Garden area, issued by the Greater London Council in their 1968 report *Covent Garden's Moving*.

The Marylebone Busway

Marylebone was the last London railway terminus to be built. It was opened in 1899 by the Great Central Railway, and has always been one of the quieter London stations. The Great Central mainline to Nottingham and Sheffield was closed down in a drawn-out process through the 1960s, leaving Marylebone to serve commuter trains to Aylesbury (running in part over the tracks of the Metropolitan line) and Banbury.

The 1950s had seen the start of Britain's motorway construction programme, and by comparison to the old-fashioned, dirty railways the private car was seen as the future. So much so, that an organization called the Railway Conversion League was formed, with the express purpose of converting railways into roads. It was felt that the gentle curves and gradients of railway formation would make excellent high-speed roads, and a number of booklets were published by the RCL into the 1970s. What they missed, however, was that roads require a wider path than railways. A piece of land wide enough for a double-track railway can only accommodate a single-carriageway road, and a four-track railway formation is not wide enough to take a dual carriageway.

Nonetheless, the RCL persisted with their misguided view that fleets of coaches running on single carriageway roads would provide the same capacity for passengers as the railways that they replaced. Whilst having some truth – coaches can drive closer together than trains, so the roads would have many low-capacity vehicles in place of a few high-capacity trains – coaches cannot drive at the same speed as trains, and would be less safe, and a single motorist who chose to drive slower would dramatically reduce the capacity of the road at a stroke.

In 1972, *The Economist* suggested that the conversion of the route into Marylebone station would provide an opportunity to perform a conversion experiment. The National Bus Company (NBC) commissioned a transport expert to prepare a report into the idea about a decade later, with the plan being to convert the station into a coach station, and run coaches through the tunnels to the north (with no other traffic being permitted). The report recommended the conversion, together with construction of about 1 km of new link road from the A40 at Northolt onto the railway formation. Coach stops would be provided at the sites of the existing stations along the route.

In parallel with the NBC study, British Rail had also commissioned a report into the feasibility of converting railways to roads, specifically looking at seven railways in the London area. Six of these were quickly dismissed on the grounds of existing heavy traffic on the railways or difficulties of conversion due to tunnels or viaducts. The Chiltern route into Marylebone was the only one that was therefore examined in detail. West of Northolt junction the benefits of conversion were seen as low, but the route east into Marylebone seemed to have a business case. Ramps would lead up from the A321 at Northolt Park onto the new road, and junctions would be provided at the A404 in Sudbury, the North Circular Road at Neasden, and the A41 at the Regent's Canal.

The tunnels between Finchley Road and Marylebone were the big problem, and the BR report noted that these would confine the traffic on the new road to private cars, or single-deck buses and coaches. The road would be 6.7 m wide, narrowing to 5.9 m under the bridge at West Hampstead, and the maximum speed would be 40 mph. BR would retain ownership of the route, and would charge the Department of Transport a toll per vehicle (known as a 'shadow toll', as there would be no toll booths or visibility of this to the road users).

The NBC report estimated the cost of conversion as being £10.3 million; the BR report reckoned on £15.7 million for a busway, and £15.9 million if private cars were to use the road. The existing train services into Marylebone would be diverted: the High Wycombe line trains into Paddington, and the Aylesbury trains would shuttle to Amersham and transfer passengers onto the Metropolitan line into Baker Street.

Unsurprisingly, the users of the services into Marylebone were not happy, and a fierce media campaign was fought. Despite some tactics seen elsewhere when railway closures were proposed – such as starting the statutory closure process during the summer holiday period when many commuters might be away and less likely to write in with objection letters – so many letters were received that the deadline had to be extended by six weeks.

The pressure continued to mount on BR as the public enquiry into the closure was due to begin. The enquiry was delayed after BR found that some of its figures were wrong, and then again on legal grounds. When it was decided that the objectors would not be able to cross-examine BR officials directly a legal challenge was mounted. Meanwhile, London Underground were expressing disquiet over the plans for the Metropolitan line to replace the Aylesbury services; the introduction of Travelcards had led to a jump in passenger numbers, and they realized that Baker Street would not have the capacity to handle commuters displaced from Marylebone.

It was about this time that BR started to change their minds. The creation of the Network SouthEast business unit, with its own distinctive branding, together with the rise in passenger numbers in the region were leading to a different view. The services out of Marylebone were rebranded as the Chiltern Line, even whilst the public enquiry into the closure was being planned. The decision was taken in April 1986 to reprieve the line, and invest in it instead of closing it down. The sale of part of the site of Marylebone station contributed towards refurbishment of the stations along the route, and most importantly, a new fleet of trains. Since then, the Chiltern Line has gone from strength to strength, and has been one of the success stories of the privatization era.

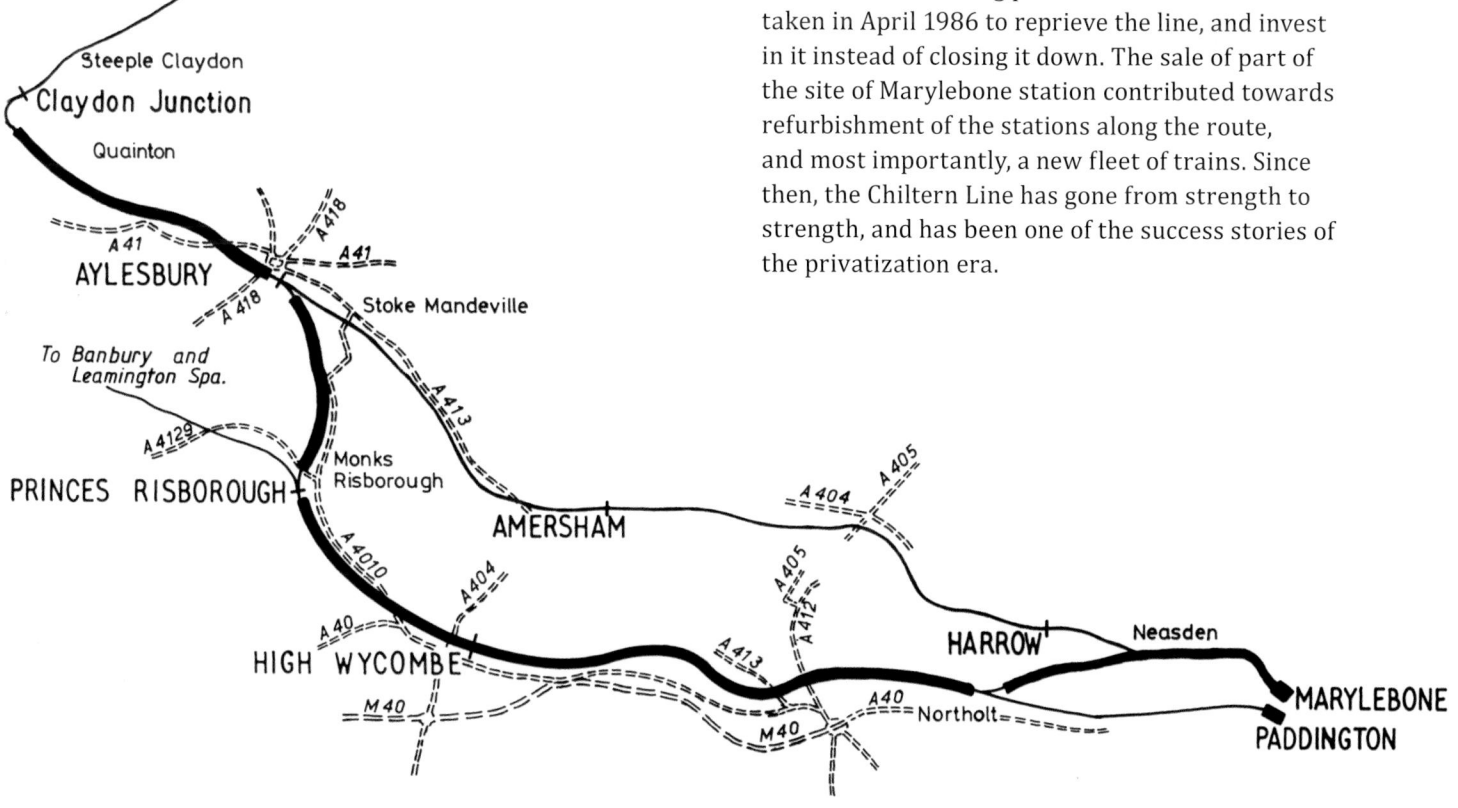

The report proposing the creation of the Marylebone busway included this map showing, in bold, the sections of railway that were felt suitable for conversion into the busway.

The Ringways

Following the demise of the post-War schemes, two decades would pass before similar proposals would be made public. The Greater London Council (the successor to the LCC) proposed a series of ring roads and radial routes around London in an attempt to tackle the traffic congestion that was increasing at a dramatic rate as car ownership increased. These plans had been started in secret by the LCC in the 1950s, and were seen as a necessary response to the growing levels of traffic congestion.

The idea was originally known as the Motorway Box, as it consisted of four motorways that formed a trapezoid box around the centre of London. To reduce the impact, the new roads would follow existing railway corridors where possible: the North, West, and South London lines between Hackney (in the north-east), via Willesden Junction, to Clapham Junction, and on to Kidbrooke (in the south-east). The eastern side had no railway to follow: instead, it would head north from Kidbrooke, crossing the Thames using the Blackwall Tunnel, and continue north back to Hackney. Connections would be made with radial motorways too.

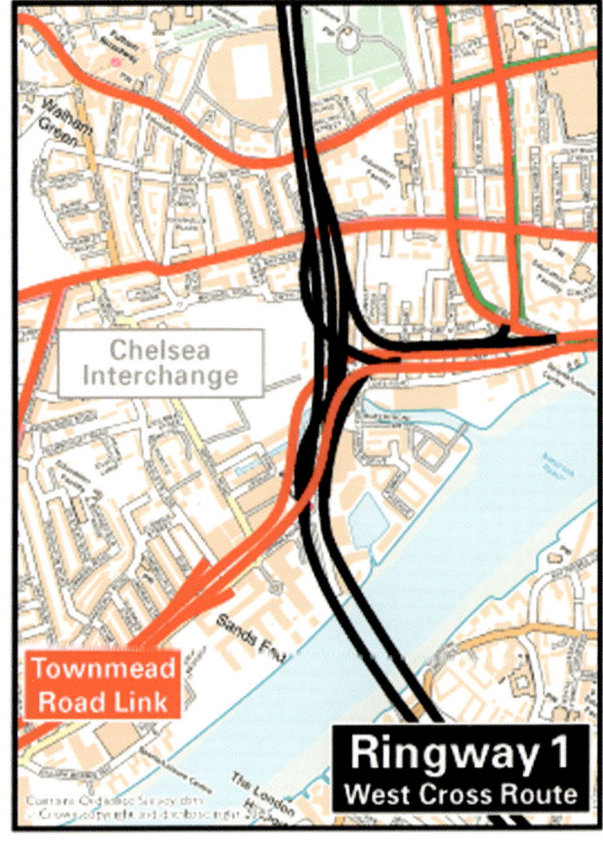

Chelsea Interchange on the edge of Chelsea Harbour, in both map (top) and isometric form (bottom). The drawing includes Lots Road power station at top left, alongside the new elevated road.

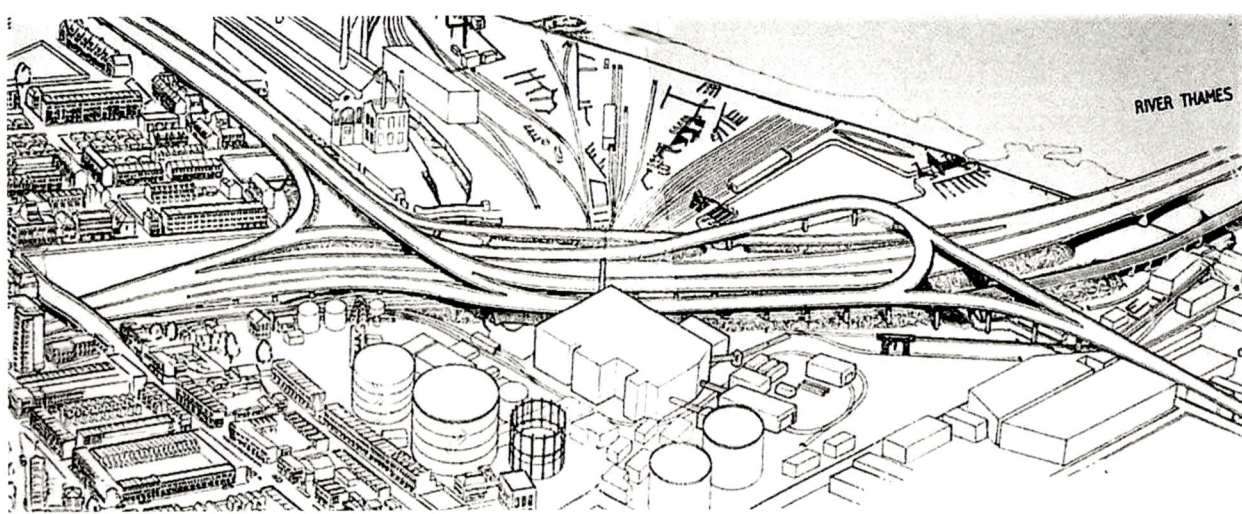

This route, known as Ringway 1, approximated to the B ring in the LCC plan, and not unexpectedly, further Ringways were planned at greater distances from London. Ringway 2 was the North and South Circular Roads, with the north side being very similar to the C ring. In the south though, the route was planned to be a little further out, but would still require significant demolition of housing and other property. Ringways 3 and 4 were planned to be even further out.

Construction work started in 1967, with the demolition of houses in North Kensington to make way for the Western Avenue Extension, known as the Westway. Since the 1930s, this had ended at Wood Lane, with London-bound traffic heading south to Shepherd's Bush Green and then following the congested Holland Park Avenue and Bayswater Road. The new extension would carry the road on a concrete viaduct all the way to Paddington and then on to join the Marylebone Road east of Edgware Road. At the western end, a section of the West Cross Route (the western side of the motorway box) was also built, running south to the Holland Park roundabout, pressed in tightly against the existing railway. The two roads met at a large roundabout, which was built with stubs on its north side ready for the northern section of the West Cross Route, which was never built.

On the opposite side of London, the East Cross Route was built in its entirety. This was, in part, because it had been planned before the Ringway scheme was developed to facilitate access to the Blackwall Tunnel, and was therefore easier to get started. It is further out from central London than any of the other sides of the motorway box, and in the mid-1960s a new line was proposed to the west of the Docklands area. However, it would have been extravagant to build both roads, and the Blackwall Tunnel route was ready to go, this was not pursued. The road was opened in 1970.

Right: The West Cross Route. The only part completed was the short stretch between Shepherd's Bush (Holland Park Roundabout) and the elevated A40 Westway.

Neither the North nor the South Cross Routes were built at all, which is unsurprising because of the amount of demolition that would have been required. The northern route would have started with a west-facing link on the A40 at Acton, running north-east to a large interchange to the east of Willesden Junction station, where the West Cross Route would start. It would then have followed the line of the North London Railway, in a cutting, as far as a large junction with the Finchley Road, roughly on the site of today's O$_2$ shopping centre. There would also be a junction with an extended M1 at Kilburn; from here to Finchley Road the route would have four carriageways.

A cut-and-cover tunnel would take the route under Belsize Park to Camden, where a double-deck elevated interchange would have changed the look of the Camden Lock Market area for ever. Continuing eastwards, two more tunnels would have been built to take the route beneath Islington and Homerton, just before it met the East Cross Route.

The southern route would have been built as a continuation of the West Cross Route, starting

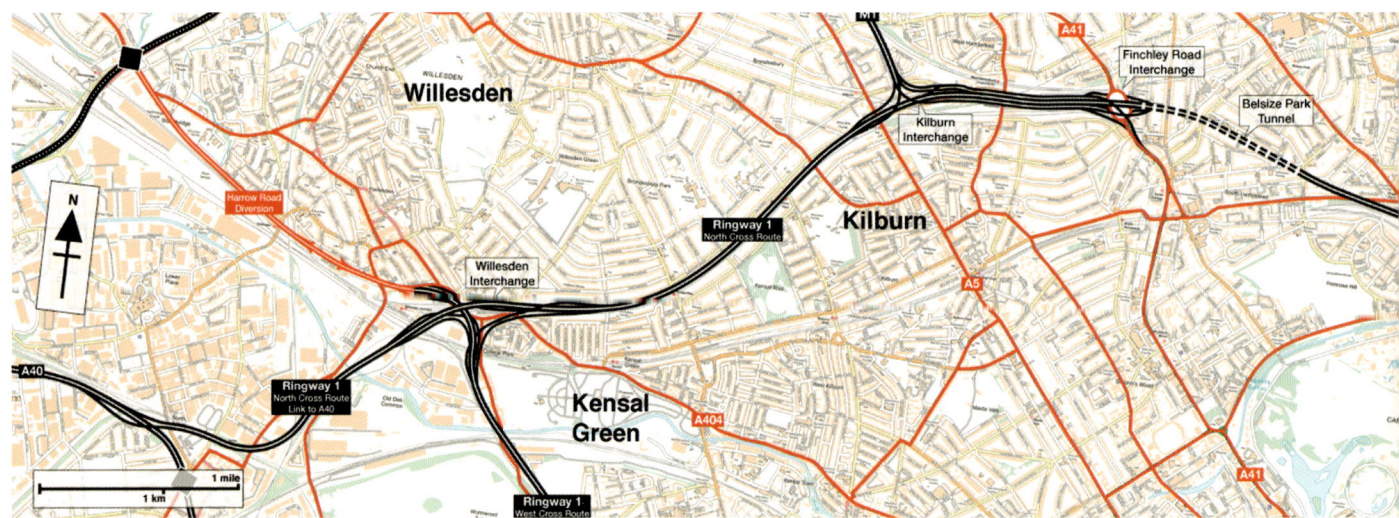

The North Cross Route

The South Cross Route

at Clapham Junction where the road would have passed beneath the railway embankments to the east of the station. After a junction in Battersea, the road would swing south-east to follow the course of the South London Line railway as far as Brixton. Here, much of the town centre would have been demolished to accommodate the motorway, running on a viaduct at sixth-floor level. Bus lay-bys would be built to allow passengers to connect with the main-line and Underground stations, but there would no connection with the local town's road network.

Following the route east, the carriageways would split to leave Denmark Hill station in the central reservation, before curving through Peckham to Lewisham. The final section would run through Blackheath to join the East Cross Route at Kidbrooke Interchange. The original plan was for a cut-and-cover tunnel under Blackheath, but this would involve demolition of every building along the line of route. A subsequent study recommended moving the route northwards, and placing it into bored tunnels that would be far more expensive, but would not damage Blackheath.

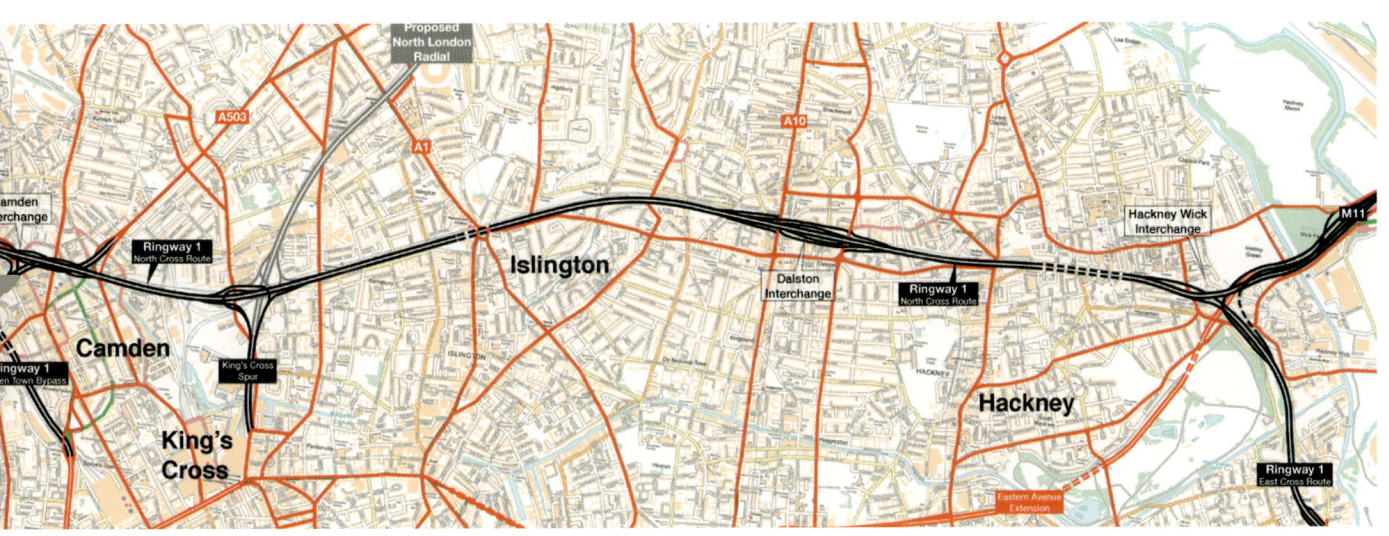

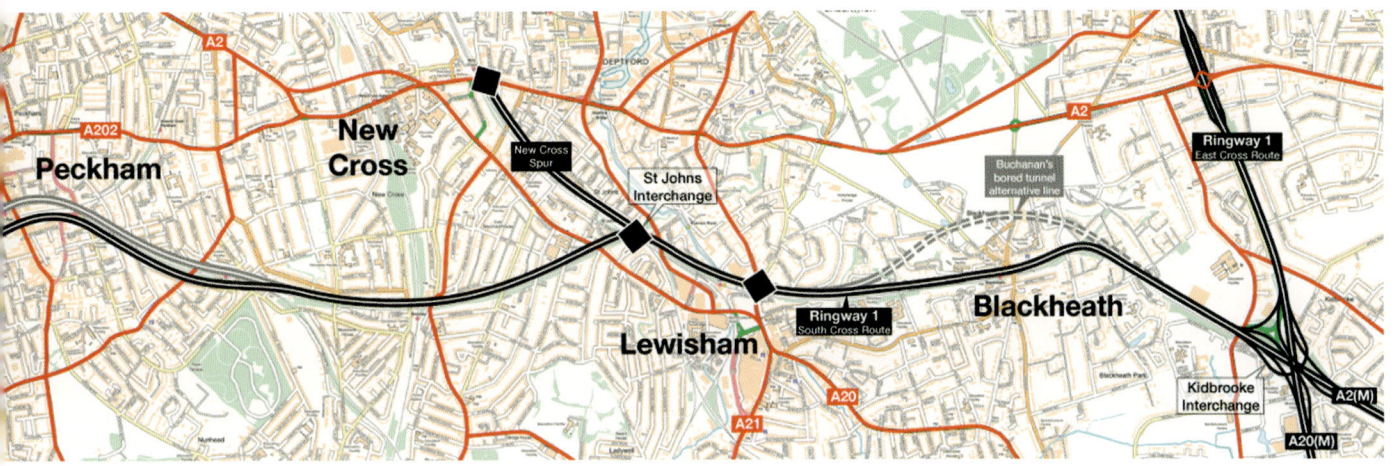

The GLC appeared to be surprised by the opposition raised to its scheme. The residents of North Kensington who lost their homes to the Westway were arguably the lucky ones: those in the streets immediately north of the new viaduct found their homes overshadowed, and bombarded with noise and pollution. By this time, those living along the routes of the other motorways that would form the rest of the box were protesting vociferously too. The GLC did not help its cause by keeping the precise routes a secret, meaning that many thousands of houses were blighted by the threat of demolition. Pressure groups were formed across the capital, dedicated to opposing the new roads — especially in the planning inquiry that was launched in 1970, and chaired by Frank Layfield Q.C. Until this was concluded, the GLC was not able to start any more construction work, even for schemes that were ready and approved, such as the continuation of the West Cross Route southwards from Holland Park.

The planning inquiry was not impressed by the GLC, which was vague about the costs of the scheme, and could not relate the evidence for the motorways to its overall strategy. The Ministry of Transport was unable to provide support, because it had been merged with the Ministry of Housing and Local Government which was overseeing the inquiry. The new Department of the Environment could not oversee the inquiry and back one side, so only questions of fact could be answered by its roads branch. Only the British Roads Federation spoke up for the motorway plans.

The recommendations of the inquiry, published in the 1972 Layfield Report, included:
- support for Ringway 1 (the motorway box);
- scrapping the southern half of Ringway 2 (the South Circular Road); and
- scrapping the western and southern sections of Ringway 3, and linking this with the MoT's South Orbital Motorway.

The latter recommendation would extend the

A model of the proposed Brixton redevelopment plan, showing how the area would be split by the elevated South Cross Route cutting across. Much of the area each side of the motorway would be rebuilt with hexagonal tower blocks. An elevated restaurant was planned above the motorway where it crossed Brixton Road (in the middle of the picture).

South Orbital Motorway, which had already been allocated the number M25. The inquiry suggested linking the western section with Ringway 3 near to Watford, and on the eastern side connecting the planned junction at Chevening with the Dartford Crossing. This would form a complete circuit around the boundary of London, and is the reason why traffic following the M25 at Junction 5 (Chevening) branches off the mainline of the road, instead of continuing straight ahead.

The biggest shock from the enquiry was the recommendation that Ringway 1 (renamed the Inner London Motorway) be constructed within 20 years. Protestors and councils across London geared themselves up for a new fight. It was quickly won through, as the Labour party opposition on the GLC decided to no longer support the scheme. In April 1973, they won the local elections, and the plans were dropped.

Not all commentators saw the Ringways as a bad idea. As late as August 1972, the *Illustrated London News* published an article comparing London unfavourably with Paris, which was busy constructing its Boulevard Périphérique around the centre of the city.[49] Their map featured all of the Ringways – not just those favoured by the Layfield inquiry, and showed how the road could provide additional car parking. A monorail would suspend beneath the road deck, although it is not clear whether this was ever part of the official plans.

It is interesting, however, to look at some of the similarities and differences to changes that were eventually made. The North Circular Road was upgraded in a piecemeal fashion over the decades, and much of it is now a dual carriageway with grade-separated junctions. The South Circular remains a patchwork of local roads that provide a poor substitute for a ring road. The main arterial road to the north-west was planned to be along the route of today's A41, whereas the M1 was actually built along the alignment of the sub-arterial route 4. The A12 uses much of the route of the arterial route 11. To the west, arterial route 1 is probably the road that has come closest to being built in the form envisaged in 1944, as it forms the M4/A4 route all of the way into Earl's Court.

The connections on the eastern side of London have always been made more difficult by the presence of the Thames, but this is also a reason that they are important: between the Blackwall and Dartford Tunnels, the only river crossing for vehicles is the Woolwich Ferry, which has limited capacity. Thamesmead has particularly poor connectivity, and there have been several schemes to provide a bridge in the vicinity.

Ringway 2 was to have an immersed-tube tunnel beneath the Thames linking Beckton with Thamesmead. The tunnel would have consisted for four separate two-lane tunnels, with changeable signs allowing the number of lanes in each direction to vary according to traffic demands. As described previously, the plans were cancelled in 1973.

Leading off the North Cross Route was a planned Camden Town By-Pass extending to a junction next to the south end of Mornington Crescent. Camden Market would have been obliterated by this new road and the character of Camden Town ruined.

London monorails

In 1967, a forward-looking booklet was published which proposed a new mode of transport for London – monorails. Written by Brian Waters for the Conservative party opposition at the Greater London Council (GLC), *Get our Cities Moving* proposed four separate monorail loops that would serve London from west to east. Each loop would have two points of interchange with adjacent loops, allowing passengers to cross London from north to south, or east to west, with minimal changes of vehicle, and no need to travel vertically any higher than the first floor of a building. The loops were laid out each with a strong north/south alignment to complement the east/west bias of the existing Underground lines.[50]

The system proposed was made by a French consortium called SAFEGE (**S**ociété **A**nonyme **F**rançaised' **E**tude de **G**estion et d' **E**ntreprises, which translates as French Limited Company for the Study of Management and Business), whose members included Michelin and Renault. The monorail cars would be suspended from overhead structures, which consisted of large box girders supported by regular pylons placed down the centre of streets. The cars would be sufficiently high above the traffic to avoid conflict, and would be propelled by rubber-tyred wheels fitted to motorized bogies running within the box girder.

Travelling at speeds of up to 40 mph, the monorail cars would be driverless. Although the images in the booklet show separate, single cars in operation, it is likely that they would be able to operate in longer multiple formations. Platforms would be at first-floor level, reached from the pavements by escalators, and it was hoped that adjacent shops would provide direct access from their first floors.

The 43 km of monorail tracks would cost an estimated £53 million to build and equip at 1967 prices, and would also bring an additional advantage in allowing street signs and lighting to be attached to the pylons, thus reducing street clutter. In practice, it appears similar to the monorail system in Wuppertal, Germany, although the SAFEGE support structure appears to be a little less intrusive than the large metal supports in Wuppertal.

It might seem surprising that the Conservative party would be proposing such an investment in public transport in the 1960s, but there was a practical motive. They believed that the monorail would replace many of the bus routes in central London, thus creating more road space for private cars (and removing the 'problem' of buses regularly stopping). However, despite taking over the leadership of the GLC later in 1967, the monorail scheme faded away after a preliminary feasibility study was carried out by Tony Ridley (who went on to become the chief executive of London Underground in the 1980s).[51] This study suggested that an overhead monorail would pose major environmental problems, which would probably make it unacceptable to the public.

Despite this though, a new monorail proposal was made in the 21st century. A British company called MonoMetro was promoting a new monorail system in Saudi Arabia; it also produced a set of concept illustrations showing their system in London. However, although it lobbied Transport for London to consider its ideas as an alternative to Crossrail, an assessment showed that it did not have a satisfactory business case.[52]

Opposite top: An illustration of how Regent's Street might appear today with the 1967 monorail scheme in place, and with TfL-branded monorail cars (although they don't look high enough above the road to clear the double-decker buses).

Opposite bottom: The map of the four monorail loops, published by the GLC in 1967, and showing how six key interchanges would allow travel across London from east to west with at most three changes.

BUS
STOP

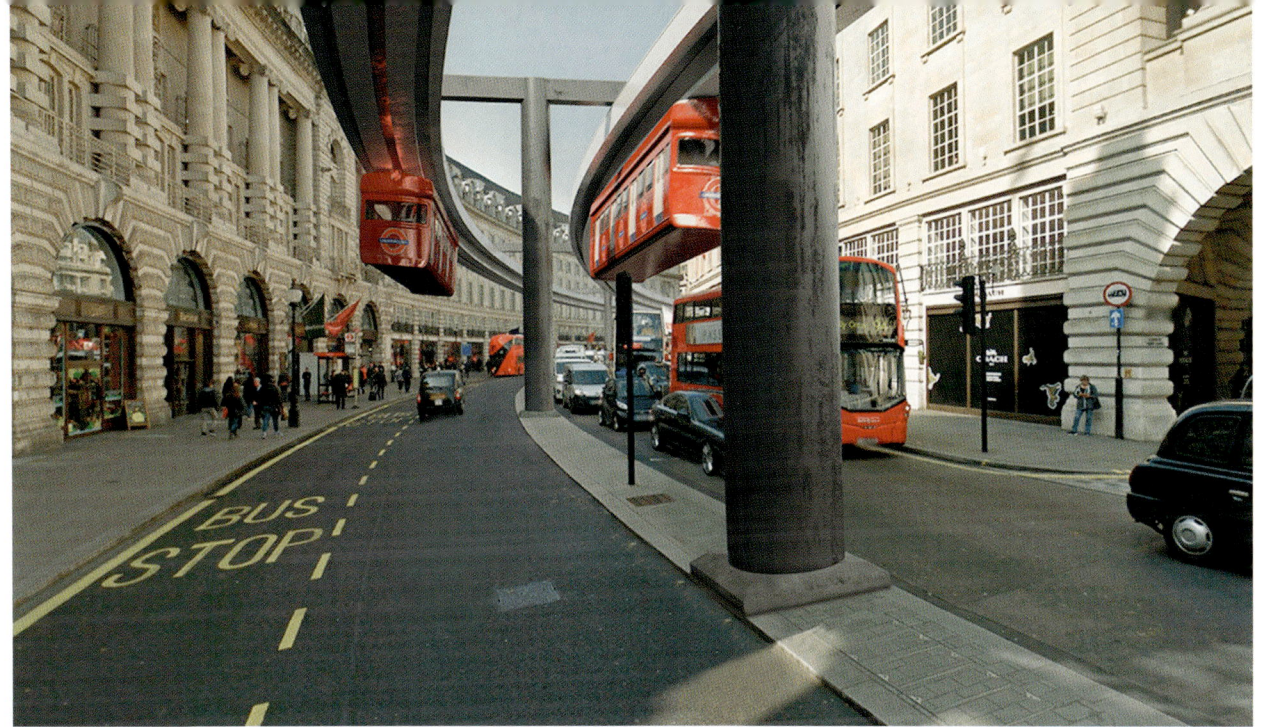

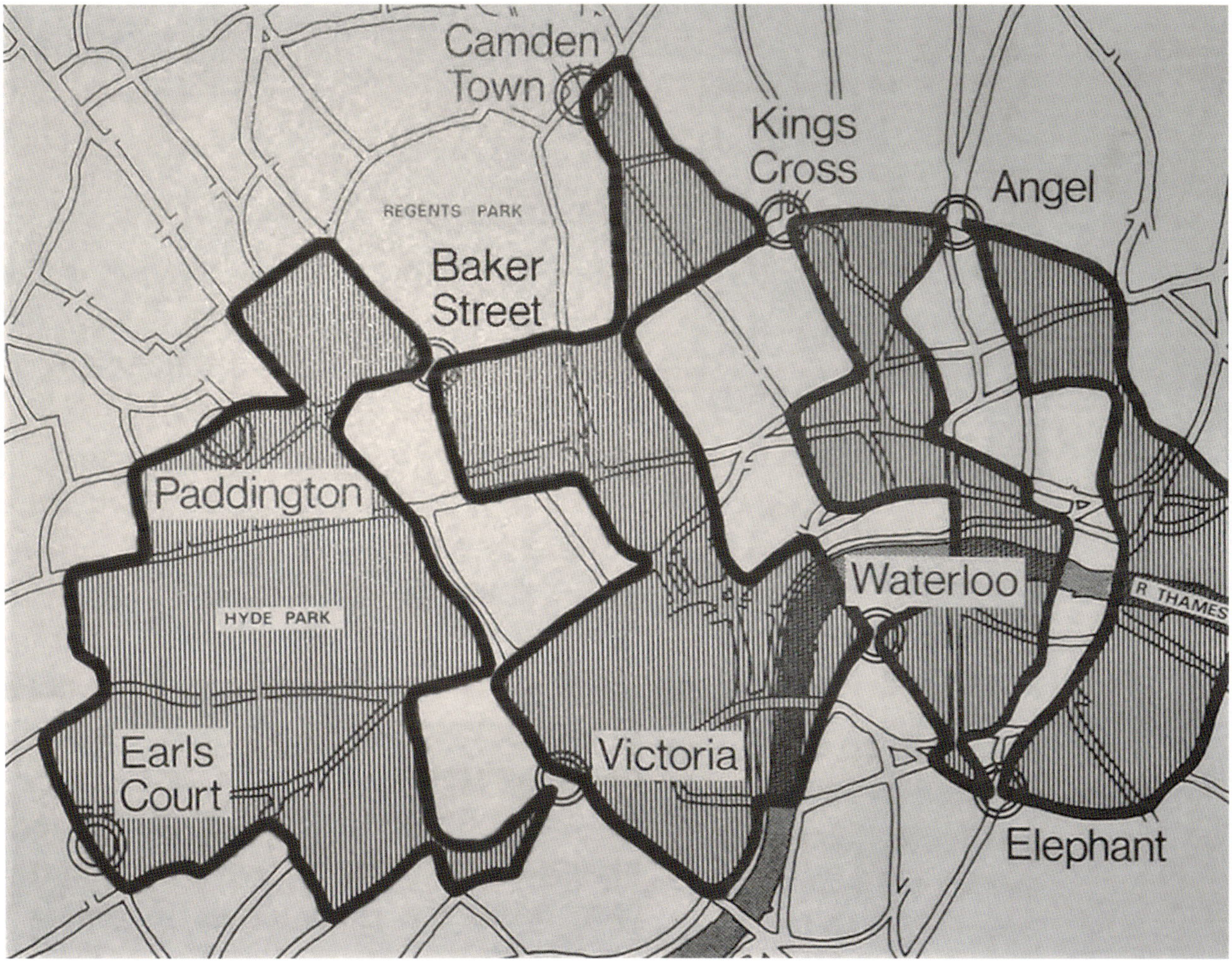
Camden
Town
Kings
Cross
Angel
REGENTS PARK
Baker
Street
Paddington
HYDE PARK
Waterloo
R THAMES
Earls
Court
Victoria
Elephant

Hammersmith Broadway redevelopment

In the late 1970s, London Transport decided to redevelop their site at Hammersmith Broadway. This consisted of the Underground station, served by the District and Piccadilly lines, and the bus station at ground level, above the tracks, marooned in a large traffic gyratory that was built at about the same time as the Hammersmith flyover. This is a long concrete viaduct, opened in 1961, on which the A4 bypasses the town centre. The gyratory itself cut off access to the bus and Underground station from the town, with subways under the road for pedestrians.

As well as the stations, the 3.7 acre site included a mix of buildings, and LT asked the architect Norman Foster to come up with a scheme that would encompass the whole area. A large amount of office accommodation was required in order to provide a rental income to LT that would help to pay for the considerable reconstruction and development work, estimated at £50 million. It would be the largest integrated office scheme in the UK at the time.[53]

Foster's proposal was for a ring of office buildings to encircle the site, with the transport facilities in the middle. The offices would be accessed from four lift cores positioned at the corners of the site. At ground floor level, car parking and delivery bays would have easy access from the roads, with an inner service road running around the edge of the site. The bus station and garage would be on a podium above this level. Above the buses would be a large piazza filling the centre of the space. This would be protected from the weather by a large lightweight roof made

of glass-fibre, held in place by tensioned steel cables. The piazza would be linked to the levels beneath by escalators, descending all the way to the Underground station below ground level. Trees would be provided in the piazza (the architectural sketches refer to "landscaped gardens", together with an ice rink, shops, and restaurants. The intention was to make Hammersmith Broadway a destination in its own right.

Above the transparent roof, the designs included a tower for a helipad. Despite the failure of helicopters as a means of city transport (see p42), architects still appeared to enjoy adding facilities to them to their developments, perhaps feeling that this would make their plans more futuristic.

To improve access to the site, the plans showed the closure of Queen Caroline Street, along the western boundary. This would remove the race-track-like traffic separating the Broadway site from the rest of Hammersmith, and provide a pedestrianized space across to the shops and St Paul's Church.

Planning permission was granted for the scheme by Hammersmith & Fulham Borough Council, and it appeared that work would be starting in late 1979 on clearing the site. However, by mid-1979, it was being reported that LT had ordered work on the scheme to cease. The developers appointed to the scheme were asking for changes, to which Foster objected. He had envisioned the development as a complete package, and did not want the concept diluted; as a result of the dispute, Foster was sacked as architect. Local residents protested to LT – one of the few instances of locals protesting in favour of a redevelopment scheme.

LT refused to comment, and by 1980 had appointed new architects to work on the redevelopment, which was now costed at £60 million. The new plans became mired in legal disputes and controversy though, and it was not until 1993 that the redevelopment was completed – to a very different design to that created by Norman Foster.

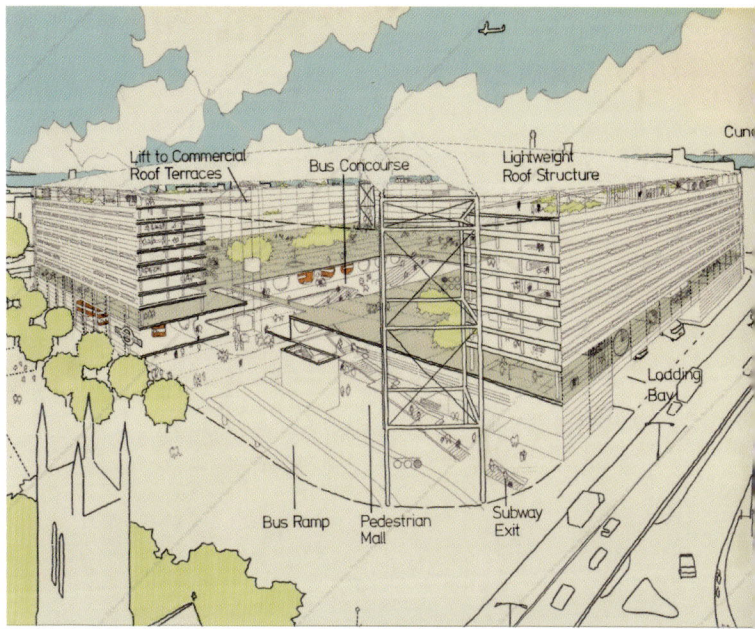

Cutaway sketches of the proposed ring of office buildings in the Norman Foster plans for Hammersmith Broadway.

Opposite: A drawing showing how the new Hammersmith Broadway development would appear from St Pauls Green, to the west of the site.

The National Gallery Extension

The north side of Trafalgar Square is occupied by the National Gallery, one of Britain's most well-known art galleries. The site to the west of the gallery was originally occupied by a department store that was destroyed by bombing during the Blitz in WWII. This site remained derelict, and was bought be the government in 1958 to be used for an extension to the gallery. Very little happened until in 1982 an architectural competition was held for the design of the new building.

Perhaps the most radical of the entries was that of Richard Rogers, whose modernist building for Lloyd's of London was under construction at the time. The proposal for the National Gallery employed a similar style, with cladding in stainless steel and many of the services and structural elements of the building on the outside. A tower, looking a bit like a UFO, would stand over the site adjacent to the existing Gallery building, whilst the main part of the site consisted of a three-storey building with a larger structure building hovering above, supported on large columns.

Rogers did not win the competition, but the winning design (by the firm of Ahrends, Burton, and Koralek) was modified to include a tower at the front. This was the design that was subsequently described by Prince Charles as 'like a monstrous carbuncle on the face of a much loved and elegant friend', and his opinion didn't change, despite a visit to the architects' office to discuss the design.[54] Planning permission was refused by Westminster Council in September 1984, and it was only when

A side profile of the design for the National Gallery Extension from Richard Rogers, clearly showing the central tower and the floating (or looming) adjacent building.

the Sainsbury brothers (of supermarket fame) offered to provide the funding for the extension. A new competition was launched, and Robert Venturi's design was chosen which, when opened in July 1991, became known as the Sainsbury Wing of the National Gallery.

The modified plans from Ahrends, Burton, and Koralek, as despised by Prince Charles.

The Thames Gateway Bridge

The East London River Crossing, proposed in 1979, would have been a high-level bridge arching across the river leaving enough space beneath for shipping, costing around £300 million. The contentious part of the plan was the road leading to it on the southern side, which would have destroyed a large portion of Oxleas Wood (a Site of Special Scientific Interest) on its way to a junction with the A2 at Falconwood. A large campaign against the crossing was started by local residents and environmentalists, and in 1993 the Government withdrew the scheme.

Eleven years later, and now named the Thames Gateway Bridge, the plans were revived. The bridge was at the same location, but without the southern link to the A2 (and now priced at £500 million). This allowed it to be seen as more of a local benefit, rather than allowing longer-distance traffic to pass through (and pollute) the area with little benefit to locals. The bridge would have dedicated public transport lanes, initially intended for buses but with a long-term suggestion of a tram network. The London Mayor at the time, Ken Livingstone, supported the scheme. In 2008, when he was replaced by Boris Johnson, the bridge was cancelled. One relic of the plan is a dead-end road stub leading across the entrance to Beckton DLR depot. This would have linked the Royal Docks Road to the bridge, but is now destined to be a fenced-off relic of what might have been.

The hiatus was now back to six years: in 2014, Transport for London revived the scheme but reduced in scale with just two lanes for road traffic. There would be additional space for public transport, with an extension of the Docklands Light Railway being a likely solution as it was already close to the north end of the bridge, and would provide a useful connection to Thamesmead. Bus lanes and a new tram network were also options. The Gallions Reach Crossing, as it was now called, has faded away since the 2016 change of Mayor, with attention instead being given to developing a tunnel further west at Silvertown. It would appear that Thamesmead will continue waiting for its link across the river.

The southern approach to the East London River Crossing would have cut through Oxleas Wood, south of Woolwich. This would have been on a similar alignment to that of Ringway 2, shown in the map here.

Opposite: Four possible options for the design of the Thames Gateway Bridge, taken from the Public Consultation document of 2003. The bridge had to provide sufficient headroom for shipping, but not interfere with the flight paths into London City Airport.

Camden Town station

The Northern line of the London Underground (LU) splits into two at Camden Town station, both northward (the Edgware and Barnet branches) and southward (the West End and City branches). This makes it a key junction at which many passengers will change trains. The original connections between the platforms are narrow passageways at the south end of the platforms, and which are still in use. The majority of passengers will use the additional subways added in 1929 when escalators replaced lifts at the station.

Since the 1990s, rising passenger numbers on the Underground have caused increased congestion. The popularity of the nearby Camden Lock Market means that the station often closes to incoming passengers at the weekends, as the two escalators and passageways simply cannot cope. In the early 2000s, LU and Jestico+Whiles Architects put forward plans to rebuild the station and significantly increase its capacity. The scheme was shown to the public in a booklet published by LU in December 2000, and was to be opened to public consultation in 2001, until the Mayor of London stated his opposition to the design.

The plans were amended and went through numerous phases of public consultation, redesign, and alterations to the building, and especially the over-site development. By the time a final design was agreed upon by LU, sixteen different variations had been considered. The new design created two separate buildings on the site, with a new pedestrian street between, parallel to Buck Street.

One of the early concept designs produced by Wilkinson Eyre Architects for the rebuilt station, with a distinctive canopy projecting forward providing a covered meeting space outside.

Another concept placed the station entrance at the north end of the site and included a thin tower harking back to some of the 1930s station designs, such as those at Osterley and Boston Manor.

The station building was to sit at the apex of the junction between Camden High Street and Kentish Town Road. The plan was to demolish this complete triangular site as far north as Buck Street, including the popular Camden Market and Electric Ballroom, as well as the United Reformed Church. The large footprint of the works was required because of the complexity of the reconstruction work and the need to keep the station open. A temporary station would have been built at the north end of the site whilst the permanent replacement would take the place of the original station, with a modern glass-fronted office and residential development would have been placed above. Unsurprisingly this £135-million-scheme was not popular with local residents and those who used these venues, and opposition was raised at the planning enquiry. In June 2005 the scheme was rejected by the Deputy Prime Minister, John Prescott, who noted that the plans "would neither enhance nor preserve the character and appearance of the conservation area".[55]

The Financial District

The Millennium Tower

Following the destruction of the Baltic Exchange by an IRA bomb in 1992, the site at 30 St Mary Axe in the City of London needed reconstruction. The initial proposal, in 1996, was for the Millennium Tower, which was designed by Foster + Partners. The tower was to have been huge: the tallest in Europe, and sixth tallest in the world, rising to 386 metres. Its 92 storeys would have provided 140,000 m^2 of floor space, for use by a mix of residential, hotel, and office space.

Double-decker lifts would be used to reach all of the floors, but the lift shafts would have been spread throughout the asymmetric footprint of the building, rather than being clustered into one main lift core. The public would be allowed up to a viewing gallery exactly 1,000 ft up (305 m). From some angles the building looked quite thin, with light passing all the way through it, and the architects emphasized the way that sunlight would continuously change as it was reflected from the curved façade.

The lack of tapering as it rose gave the illustrations of the tower a rather looming bulk, and it was not surprising that a building so much taller than anything else in London received much opposition. The Commissioners of English Heritage stated that it "represents such a quantum leap in terms of scale, height and bulk that it would overwhelm the quintessential character of the capital". Possibly the biggest problem was the opposition from the Civil Aviation Authority,

The sheer height of the Millennium Tower would have overshadowed the whole of the City of London.

fearing that it would interfere with flight paths into Heathrow Airport.⁵⁶ A redesign of the building with fewer floors was also rejected, but (after the site had been sold to new owners) Foster + Partners created a new design. This was the iconic building for Swiss Re, which was quickly nicknamed 'The Gherkin' because of its distinctive curved shape. This was approved, including by English Heritage.⁵⁷

The Minerva Tower

Designed by Grimshaw Architects, the Minerva Tower was planned for a site adjacent to Aldgate Underground station, at the edge of the City of London. Its mirrored façade would have given it a very striking look, compounded by the asymmetric design. This was described as being like four open books with their spines erect facing one another – and each tower would have a different height. The shortest was 92m, then 100m and 198m, with the tallest at 217m, topped by a spire taking it to around 250m high.

The scheme had grown from an original plan for a 14-storey building, which the owning property group Minerva decided to scale up to 35 floors. In 2001, they then asked Grimshaw to completely redesign the scheme to accommodate 52 floors, leading to the 'mirrored book' design'. As with most modern London skyscrapers, public viewing areas and a restaurant were to have been provided.

Planning permission was obtained without the need for an enquiry, but it proved harder than expected for Minerva to find tenants to lease the 1·4 million square feet of office space. In 2006 the plans were abandoned, and a smaller building called St Botolph's House, also designed by Grimshaw, was constructed on the site.

The unusual floorplan and mirrored glass façade of the Minerva Tower would have given it an impressive lightness for its size, although such computer-generated illustrations tend to make new buildings look better than they appear in real life.

87

The Pinnacle

This was to have been a 63-storey tower 288 m high, designed by Kohn Pedersen Fox Associates, and located on Bishopsgate, opposite the junction with Threadneedle Street. The original plan was for it to be 19 metres higher, but the height was reduced after concerns were raised about its proximity to the flight path for London City Airport.[58]

It was to be called The Bishopsgate Tower, but was known informally as the 'Helter-skelter tower' because of the proposed spiralling, tapering shape. Construction work started in 2006, with the existing buildings on the site being demolished, and the following year the site and planned building was sold to new investors and renamed The Pinnacle. By 2012 the concrete lift core had been built up to the seventh-floor level. Unfortunately, the recession that started in 2008 meant that there was little interest from commercial tenants. Together with a legal argument with the contractors, this caused work to cease.[59]

The site was subsequently sold on again, and although initial plans were to complete the building, the new owners decided to demolish the part-completed work (which had been nicknamed The Stump) and construct a new building. Known as Twenty-Two Bishopsgate, it is factionally shorter at 278 m, and has a simpler design than The Pinnacle, which has reduced costs in part by losing the expensive (and expansive) double-layered glass panels.

The elevated angle of this illustration reduces the apparent height of The Pinnacle, but it would still have dominated the City from many angles.

Battersea Power Station

Since its turbines stopped spinning in 1983, Battersea Power Station has been one of London's longest-running redevelopment schemes. The site has been sold multiple times, with each new owner promising bold and imaginative uses for the iconic building. It has only been in recent years that work has progressed, and at the time of writing is nearing completion. The site comprises the power station building, designed by Giles Gilbert Scott, plus a large amount of land around it.

A couple of the more dramatic proposals are described below.

1998 – The Green Bird

One of the strangest buildings proposed for London in recent years was the Green Bird skyscraper. Green Bird would have been enormous – 442 m high, with 83 storeys. However, its most distinctive feature was its shape. It was designed by the Prague-based architects Future Systems, who specialized in curvy structures (described as 'zoomorphic').

The best description of the tower would be multi-coloured and phallic, with the tower gently curving towards the south-east. Concept illustrations show that it would include a bridge across the Thames, landing on the north bank next to the Churchill Gardens estate. The shape was intended to reduce its resistance to wind,

The Green Bird building is probably the most unusual design in this book, both for the shape and the colours. Its construction would have required the complete obliteration of the power station building.

The Eco-Dome would have retained the power station building, but completely overshadowed it with the enormous glass chimney intended to provide natural ventilation for the new office space.

and the building would be strengthened by an external steel lattice structure. Internally, it would be divided into seven sub-buildings (one underground) that would have different uses, such as apartments, offices, and an hotel.

The design was intended to be very low in energy usage, with solar cells on the exterior to generate electricity. A natural ventilation system would significantly reduce the need for conventional air-conditioning.

2008 – The Eco-Dome

In 2008 the then owners, Real Estate Opportunities, unveiled their plans for the site. The architect was Rafael Viñoly, who proposed using the power station building as a shopping centre, together with a smaller power station that would use biomass and waste as fuel. The most eye-catching feature of the scheme was the eco-dome to the east, which was to be topped by a 300-metre-high glass chimney, which would dwarf those of the original power station. The dome would contain environmentally friendly offices, ventilated by the air pulled up through the chimney and removing the need for air-conditioning.[60]

The scheme was not well-received, with the London Mayor describing the chimney as 'an inverted toilet-roll holder'. A redesign replaced the single dominant chimney with several smaller towers, and planning permission was granted by Wandsworth Council in 2010. It was not a good time for major property development schemes though, with finance being hard to raise in the aftermath of the financial crisis of 2008. Despite several efforts to secure the estimated £5·5 billion required for the scheme, the money was not forthcoming and in late 2011 the developers went into administration.

The Garden Bridge

Probably the highest profile project of the 21st century that was never built in London was the Garden Bridge. Originally the idea of the actress Joanna Lumley[61] in 1998, it received significant support from Boris Johnson, once he became Mayor of London. The design was created by Thomas Heatherwick, who was also responsible for the New Routemaster bus in London. Heatherwick had already been approached by Lumley when she wrote to Johnson in 2012 asking for his support.

The bridge was intended to cross the Thames between Waterloo and Blackfriars Bridges, arriving on the north bank at Temple station where it would link to the existing terrace on the station roof. It would have been 366 m long and 30 m wide, supporting a verdant, tree-planted garden along its length. The bridge structure would be clad in copper sheeting, and would have two piers in the river, positioned asymmetrically (one closer to the north bank). The piers would have an organic look, resembling trees growing from the water. Over 270 trees and 2,000 shrubs would be planted, with paths winding through connecting the banks.

The bridge was promoted by, and funding raised by a charity called the Garden Bridge Trust. A company of the same name was to be the bridge's owner. Planning permission was granted in 2014, but conditional upon the maintenance costs of the bridge being underwritten. The Greater London Authority, led by Johnson, agreed to this.

The project was controversial for a number of reasons. Where the bridge reached the southern bank, around 30 mature plane trees would need to be felled; trees which were planted in the 1960s as a memorial to those who had died in the Second World War. The bridge would be privately owned,

On the north bank of the Thames the Garden Bridge was intended to land adjacent to Temple Underground station, taking over some of the rooftop terrace for the access stairs. This illustration shows the copper cladding on the underside of the bridge.

Local residents were upset at the loss of the plane trees on the south bank that would have been caused by the Garden Bridge, seen here crossing the existing pedestrian walkway to an elevated platform from which stairs would descend.

rather than being a public facility, and so would be closed between midnight and 6 AM, and on up to twelve days of the year when it would be used to host private functions. The use of video and mobile phone surveillance was also seen as objectionable.

The ever-increasing costs of the bridge were another big concern, together with plans for finding the money. The original estimate was £60 million, but by 2016 this had risen to £175 million. The hope had been that it would be paid for through donations by the public and philanthropists (who had already provided over £83 million), but this increase caused the Mayor to seek public funding. He arranged for Transport for London (for which the Mayor is the Commissioner) to pay £30 million, and convinced the Department for Transport to contribute the same.[62] The Mayor even flew to California with two aides for 24 hours to visit the headquarters of Apple to see if they would be persuaded to foot the entire bill in exchange for the naming rights to the bridge. Apple declined.[63]

The London elections of 2016 saw Sadiq Khan become Mayor of London that May. He soon commissioned an investigation into the decision-making around the project, and in July ordered work on the bridge to cease. No more public money was to be spent, although much of the funding from TfL had already been used by this point. The National Audit Office also reviewed the funding via the Department for Transport, and concluded that there was a significant risk that the project represented poor value for money.[64] The following year, the London Assembly reviewed the finances more generally, and stated that the bridge would now cost over £200 million, much of which would need to come from public funds, and that it was unlikely that the project would secure the money for the ongoing maintenance and operational costs.[65]

On 28 April 2017 Khan wrote to the Garden Bridge Trust to formally withdrawn the financial guarantee for the maintenance costs. As a result of this, the planning permission was no longer valid, and on 14 August the Trust announced that the project would be abandoned, having spent around £43 million of public money by this point.[66]

The Cross-River Tram

In 2001, the London Mayor announced a public consultation into a new tram for London to link Peckham, Brixton, Camden, and King's Cross, with a route length of just over 10 miles (depending on the particular route chosen). The cost was estimated to be around £600 million. The overall view was positive, and Transport for London began work to plan a suitable route. This was published in draft in 2006, and put out to another consultation.

Named the Cross River Tram (CRT), the central section would link Euston and Waterloo stations via Holborn and Aldwych. To the north it would loop into Camden, and south of Waterloo separate branches would reach out to Brixton and Peckham. The expectation was that the route would use tram vehicles similar to those in use in Croydon, introduced in 1999.

The plans showed the trams terminating along the western side of Camden Town station. From here they would run south, past Mornington Crescent station, where a branch would turn left to reach St Pancras station. Crossing underneath via Goods Way, the route would end between St Pancras and King's Cross, with the possibility of looping back north to serve the developments north of King's Cross.

The main route would follow Eversholt Street alongside Euston station, continuing straight along through Tavistock and Russell Squares to Holborn, and then down Kingsway to Aldwych. Here it would curve right to reach Waterloo Bridge, after which it would follow Waterloo Road. The Brixton branch would branch right, and travel via Lambeth North and Oval stations to Stockwell and Brixton. The branch to Peckham would continue ahead from Waterloo to St George's Circus and Elephant & Castle before following the Walworth Road, cutting across Burgess Park, to Peckham.

The tram was seen as providing a more reliable mode of transport than buses, as well as drawing passengers from already-congested sections of the Underground, such as the Northern line between Stockwell and Euston. Burgess Park, on the Peckham branch, was the closest area to central London with almost no public transport, and so would be improved by the new route. Peckham was also poorly served, for although it had several railway stations, they were not on lines heading directly for central London.

Residents at the southern end of the route were more in favour than those at the north. In particular, there was a lot of opposition in Camden, with fears of disruption during building and traffic congestion when operational. Residents even expressed concern that the tram would allow drug-dealers from Peckham to come to Camden. As a result, Camden Council raised formal objections to the scheme, and in July 2007 the Mayor announced that it might be split into two. The initial focus would be on constructing the southern branches as far as Waterloo, with phase 2 being the sections northwards to be built subsequently.

Problems arose with the planned locations for the tram depots. The proposed site north of King's Cross had objections from both Camden Council and the landowner, who felt that this would jeopardize the redevelopment potential. Another possible site was south of Peckham Rye station, but there was vociferous opposition to local residents, as well as a planning inquiry report that looked unfavourably on this suggestion.

In 2008 the cost of the scheme was estimated at £1·3 billion, but with a 2:1 benefit:cost ratio. However, the funding was not forthcoming from the Government, and there was also a mayoral election. The new mayor, Boris Johnson, announced a review of the scheme in May, and in November this resulted in an announcement from TfL that the tram would not be built. Since then, there have been occasional suggestions that the project be revived, but the current Mayor has declined, citing improvements to the services on the Northern and Victoria lines which have increased the public transport capacity on the north-south axis across central London.

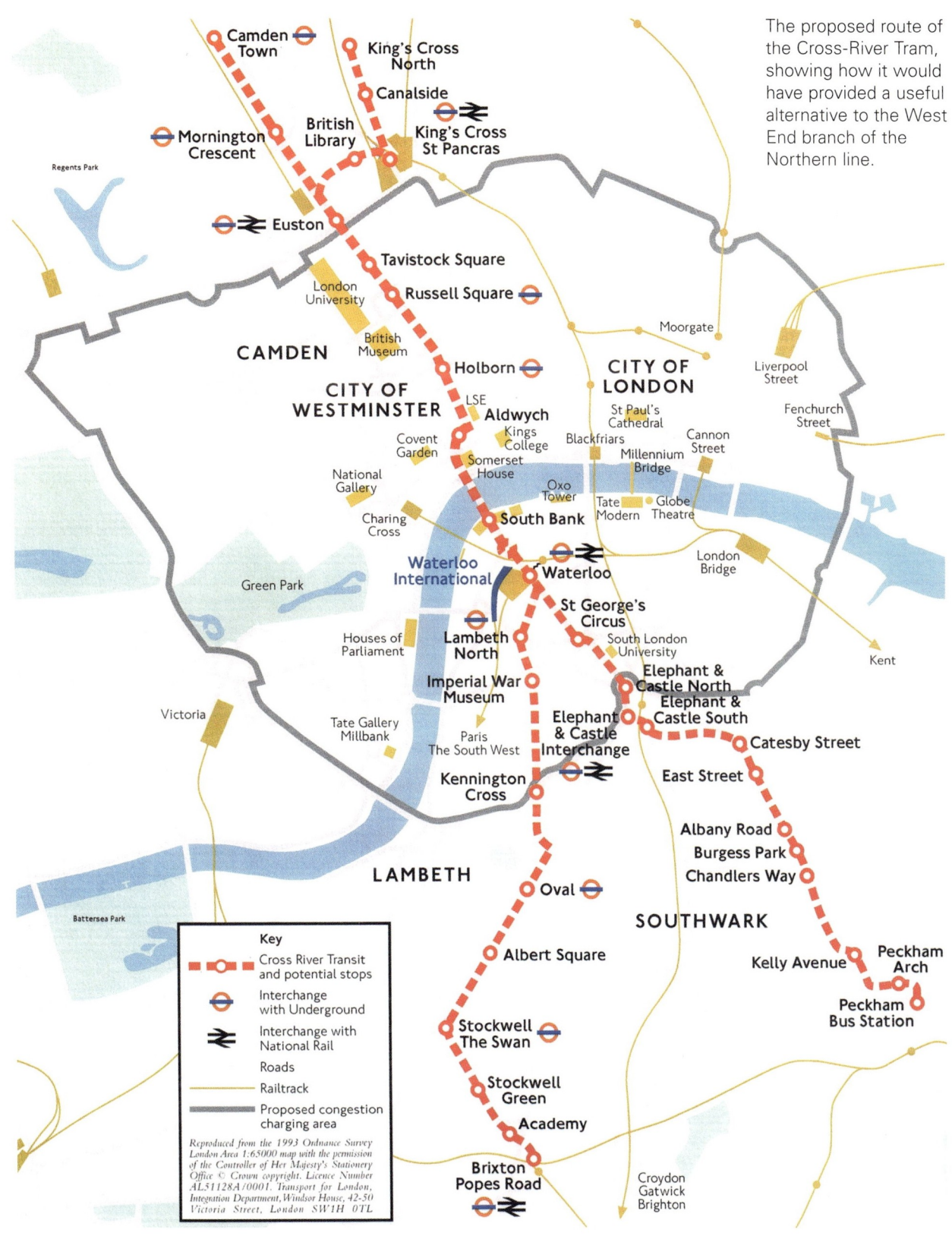

The proposed route of the Cross-River Tram, showing how it would have provided a useful alternative to the West End branch of the Northern line.

Notes

1. *The Times*, 17 October 1825.
2. *The Times*, 27 July 1891.
3. *The Times*, 29 June 1909.
4. *The Times*, 18 November 1910.
5. *The Graphic*, 5 August 1911.
6. *The Times*, 15 November 1920.
7. Engineering Timelines: Waterloo Bridge
8. Gattie, A., *How to Improve London's Transport* (London Chamber of Commerce 1910)
9. *The Motorway Achievement: Building the Network in Southern and Eastern England* (2007)
10. *The Times*, 9 February 1929.
11. *Proposed London Underground Goods Tube Railway: Report of the Committee appointed to consider and report upon the commercial aspect of the Scheme*, 6 November 1925.
12. Letters between Sir Ralph Wedgwood (Chairman of the LNER) and Robert Selbie, 12 and 20 September 1927.
13. *The Times*, 6 October 1932.
14. Press release from the GLC, 13 February 1973.
15. "London 2026 A.D. – this is all in the air" by Montague Black.
16. *The Times*, 18 June 1931.
17. *The Sphere*, 14 October 1916.
18. *The Charing Cross Bridge*, Arthur Keen (1930)
19. *The Opening of Waterloo Bridge*, London County Council (1945)
20. *The Port of London and the Thames Barrage* (Swan Sonnenschein & Co. 1907)
21. *The Festival of Britain: A Land and Its People*, by Harriet Atkinson (Bloomsbury Publishing, 2012)
22. *South Bank New Town* in *Architectural Review* (October 1966)
23. *Le Festival et son impact urbanistique* in *Mémoire(s), identité(s), marginalité(s) dans le monde occidental contemporain* (2019)
24. *Architect's Journal*, 18 December 1997
25. *The Times*, 8 May 1951.
26. *The Times*, 18 December 1952.
27. *The Times*, 16 June 1954.
28. *BBC News*, 16 January 2013.
29. *The High Paddington Scheme*, Journal of the Royal Society of Arts (3 April 1953)
30. *Ibid.*
31. The new plan was published as part of *The City of London: A record of destruction and survival* (Architectural Press, 1951).
32. *Hansard*, 2 July 1958.
33. *The Times*, 12 January 1960.
34. *Underways applied to London's traffic transport problems*, A.E.T. Matthews (1972)
35. *Tunnel Motorways: City Centres*, A.E.T. Matthews (Fifth World Meeting of the International Road Federation, London, 1966)
36. Letter from the Parliamentary Secretary to Sir Ronald Russell, M.P.
37. *Roads in Tunnel*, GLC (December 1973)
38. *London Pedway*, Joshua Ricketts (https://joshuaricketts.wordpress.com/portfolio/london-pedway/)
39. *The Pedway: Elevating London* (documentary, dir. Chris Bevan Lee, 2013).
40. gilbertscott.org/the-classical-foreign-office
41. *Hansard* vol. 164, Commons: 8 July 1861
42. *The Builder*, 26 March 1904.
43. *Ibid.*
44. *The Times*, 13 July 1964
45. *The Times*, 20 July 1965
46. *The Times*, 2 December 1965
47. *The Times*, 23 December 1965
48. *Ibid.*
49. *Illustrated London News*, 1 August 1972.
50. *Commercial Motor*, 17 March 1967
51. *Engineering in Perspective: Lessons for a Successful Career*, Tony Ridley (World Scientific Publishing 2017)
52. Mayor's Question Time, 17 October 2007.
53. *London Passenger Transport*, June 1977.
54. *The Independent*, 30 May 2014
55. BBC News, 21 June 2005.
56. *The Independent*, 31 January 1997
57. *London High*, Herbert Wright (Frances Lincoln Ltd, 2006)
58. https://www.designbuild-network.com/projects/the-pinnacle/
59. *Architects Journal*, 10 April 2013.
60. *The Guardian*, 20 June 2008.
61. *The Independent*, 3 March 2018.
62. *The Guardian*, 13 February 2016.
63. *The Guardian*, 16 July 2019
64. *Investigation: The Department for Transport's funding of the Garden Bridge*, National Audit Office, 11 October 2016.
65. *The Garden Bridge – Executive Summary*, London Assembly, April 2017.
66. BBC News, 13 February 2019.